D1308993

SOLIHULL PUBLIC LIBRARY

This book is the property of Solihull Public Library. Failure to return it before the below mentioned date will result in a minimum fine of £250 AND/OR a three-month prison sentence AND/OR compulsory self-flagellation with a Reliant Robin steering wheel cover AND/OR commital to the nearest funny farm after the above mentioned penalty has deprived you of what's left of your marbles. This book may bear a passing resemblance to a similar book misappropriated from Huddersfield Public Library and, prior to that, W.H. Smiths. It is *entirely* coincidental, if you get our drift. So just watch it, all right. Schtum!

To be returned by:

17 DEC 1983	2 MAY 1985	30 NOV 1985
17. DEC. 1983	23 MAI	
TIRS 12/12/83	13 JUN 85	8 JAN
20. 1984	25 JUN 1985	2
20. AUG 1984	19 SEP 1985	10 OCT 1986
	21 OCT 1985	
1984	26 OCT 1985	
1984		

ADULT LIBRARY HOURS
Daily 9 a.m. – 8 p.m. Saturday 9 a.m. – 5 p.m.

Books that have been exposed to any infectious disease must be returned to the Environmental Health Department

Also in Arrow by Jasper Carrott

A Little Zit on the Side
Sweet 'n' Sour Labrador

Arrow Books Limited
62–65 Chandos Place, London WC2N 4NW

An imprint of Century Hutchinson Ltd

London Melbourne Sydney Auckland
Johannesburg and agencies throughout the world

First published by Arrow 1986

© Jasper Carrott 1986

Design by Alex Evans and Zoltan Marfy
Photographs by Mike Prior
Illustrations by David Stotan and Tim Watts
of Spitting Image

This book is sold subject to the condition that it shall not, by
way of trade or otherwise, be lent, resold, hired out, or
otherwise circulated without the publisher's prior consent in
any form of binding or cover other than that in which it is
published and without a similar condition including this
condition being imposed on the subsequent purchaser

Photoset by Rowland Phototypesetting Ltd
Bury St Edmunds, Suffolk
Printed and bound in Great Britain by
Anchor Brendon Limited, Tiptree, Essex

ISBN 0 09 947560 X

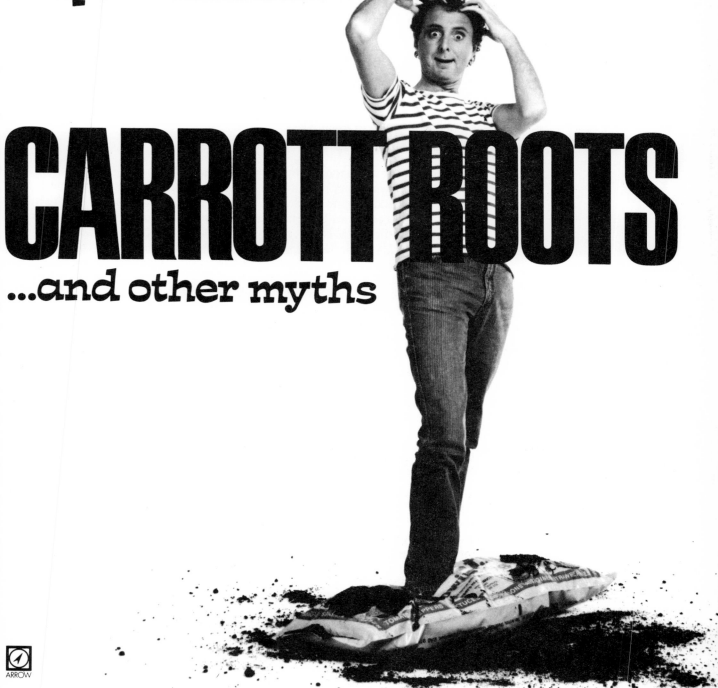

Jasper Carrott

CARROTT ROOTS

...and other myths

ARROW

A NOTE TO MY SPONSORS

A large number of business organizations have given me a lot of money to sponsor this book on the condition that I mention them somewhere in the text.

This is their mention.

Thanks, suckers.

A NOTE ABOUT HUMOUR

It has frequently been pointed out that humour is a highly personal and subjective experience. What one person may find hilarious, the next may regard as silly, boring – or even offensive. Similarly, some of the situations, characters, and anecdotes contained in this volume may, while raising a smile with Reader A, utterly fail to appeal to Reader B, not because he is a duller or more discriminating person – he is simply different from the rest of us. 'I don't think that's funny,' he may say. Or *'That's a joke*?' Maybe even 'How could they ask £3.50 for this bit of old tat?'

To this reader I would like to apologize on behalf of myself, the publisher and anybody else who has had anything else to do with it. Yes, we're all very, very sorry. We tried – God knows, we tried – but if it hasn't worked for you, well, we all feel very badly indeed about it. I mean, you should have seen the stuff we had to throw out! Personally, I don't know what to say to you beyond once again craving your forgiveness from the bottom of my heart. Have you tried Les Dawson? Now *there's* a funny man. What more can I say. Except, well, sorry . . .

A NOTE ABOUT THE PUBLISHERS

I would like to express my profound gratitude to the publishers of this book. A lot of people think that all book publishers do is sit around thinking, 'I know, why don't we get that Carrott wallah to write us another book,' and then go back to sleep until it's time to count the money coming in. The truth, of course, is very different – publishers do a lot more than that. For instance, they go round picking up all the bits of paper in the street in case they might be five-pound notes. And they do, oh, lots and lots of other things really and, well, it's very hard work counting money and, well, that's why they sleep a lot – because the work's so hard. Blimey! I bet I would sleep much longer than they do after counting because I'm not nearly as well trained as they are. Phew! Who'd be a publisher, eh? I know I wouldn't want to be, all that counting, phew, wouldn't get me at it, a right mug's job that, counting –

not for me anyway. Sore fingers and everything, all that sleeping, count me out John, know what I mean? Someone must have seen them coming, too right, am I glad they didn't see me! I can only count up to a million anyway, that is, before I fall asleep and –

Publisher's note: Mr Carrott wanted to go on for several pages in this vein but, because we are aware of our public responsibilities, we felt it advisable to stop it here.

ILLUSTRATIONS - A TECHNICAL NOTE

Many of the photographs in this book were conceived, commissioned, planned, styled, executed and developed *specifically* for *Carrott Roots*. While to the untutored eye, they may appear simple, straightforward even, each of them is the result of years of training in the theory, practice and art of creative photography. Our photographer would like you to know that it really is not as easy as it looks – the lighting, for instance, can be an absolute pig to set up if you're just some cowboy with a box camera fresh from art school and as for the sets! Nightmare city, darling. So don't go around thinking that you could have done just as well because, unless your name happens to be David Bailey, you jolly well couldn't.

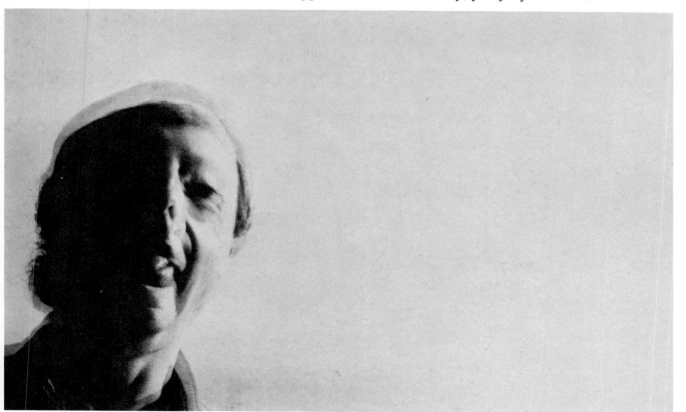

INTRODUCTION

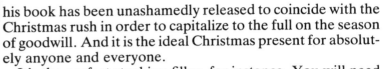his book has been unashamedly released to coincide with the Christmas rush in order to capitalize to the full on the season of goodwill. And it is the ideal Christmas present for absolutely anyone and everyone.

It's the perfect stocking-filler, for instance. You will need to roll it up into a tube it's true, but that's why it hasn't got a hard cover – so you can cram it into a sock.

Children will love it. It's got lots of pictures and *very* big print (which also makes it ideal for opticians' waiting-rooms). Whatever the age of your child, he or she is catered for. Cartoons, strawberry-flavoured printers' ink, plenty of blank spaces to draw on – nothing has been left to chance.

If you're an intellectual, you are no doubt just about to replace this book on the sales rack. Hold it! This could be the exercise in subliminal self-enlightenment you've been searching for since Carl Jung met Sigmund Freud. Just flip through the pages and consider the secret, enigmatic references to universal consciousness, the power of body, mind and synchronicity. Hooked? Of course you are.

Carrott Roots is also the perfect gift for the person you can never think of anything to get for. They'll never expect this! And you can be pretty sure that no one else will have the nerve to give them this over-priced segment of literary musak.

Don't like somebody? Give them the perfect insult. Boy, when they realize the relationship has sunk to this level, the only thing you have to worry about is if they send it back.

Think the world of somebody? Send them the book for crying out loud! But first be sure to purchase the misprint edition where the price reads £399.95. These are quite rare, but not as rare as copies I haven't signed.

It is also, of course, the ultimate coffee table book as the cover will stand most hot drinks. In fact, while you're at it, why not buy a set of six as table mats?

So you see this book will just about solve Christmas for everybody – it's a bible, companion, fly-swat, and note pad.

If you count all the words in the book and divide by ten, you have the number of days in a year.

If you count all the chapters, you have the number of months in a year.

And if you count all the dots over the 'i's, you're not fooling anyone, including the store detective who knows you're biding your time before stuffing it up your sleeve.

I know, I was that soldier.

JASPER CARROTT

ARROW
PUBLICATIONS
A division of Century/Hutchinson Ltd

Brookmount House, 62-65 Chandos Place,
Covent Garden, London WC2N 4NW
Telephone: 01-240 3411 Telex 261212
Cables Literarius London W1

Distribution Tiptree Book Services Limited
Tiptree, Colchester, Essex CO5 0SR
Telephone Tiptree 816362 Telex 99487
Overseas Melbourne, Sydney, Auckland
Johannesburg and agencies throughout the world.

Dear Jasper

Thanks for the concept sheet for the book which we all think is absolutely _amazing_ - you've done it again, Jasp!!!

One or two teensy weensy questions of balance and taste occurred to us and I thought it might be helpful to give general, informal guidelines as to what is regarded as good, strong satire round here and what we see as 'going too far'. Of course, if you want to 'go too far', that's absolutely cool with us - _we're_ not into censorship, no way - but you may possibly find there's what we call a 'negative sales shakedown'. In layman's terms, it means you sell bugger all copies!!!!

So basically it's all down to you, Jasp - you're the writer!

By the way, I couldn't help spotting that there weren't any Esther Rantzen jokes on your list. Was this a typing error? We always like to have at least one or two Esther Rantzen jokes in our humour books - for some reason, the punters really seem to go for them. Let me know if we can help there - we have a few E.R. gags filed on the computer so maybe I could punch one or two up for you???

Best,

DIRECTORS
Anthony Cheetham (Chairman)
Rosemary Cheetham
Peter Lavery
Stephen Lenaerts
John Mottram

Gail Rebuck
Peter Roche
Roger Smith
Richard Tucker

IMPRINTS
Arrow Books
Arena
Sparrow Books
Hamlyn Paperbacks
Zenith
Beaver Books

DISTRIBUTORS FOR
Geographia Maps
Nicholson Guides
Virgin Books
Hippo

Registered office number 280357 England
Although every care is taken of MSS and other documents while in our possession, we can accept no responsibility for any loss or damage thereto

POSSIBLE IDEAS FOR THE BOOK

— Not sure about this. Will it encourage our younger readers to do naughties themselves. If you must, do it. BUT KEEP IT CLEAN.!!!

'Behind the bike shed' — some childhood memories

Balance, Jasper !!! Replace with Gerald Kaufmann ???

*

Emmanuelle meets ~~Sir Keith Joseph~~

*

A brilliant sketch about trying to buy <u>The Joy of Gay Sex</u>
at W.H.Smiths

FORGET IT !!

*

A searing <u>News of the World</u> exposé of the private life
of Prince William

Sex + royal family = big trouble with the wholesalers. Is it worth it ?

*

✓✓ GREAT

How record companies rip off starving comedians

*

✓✓✓ GREAT !!!

How the BBC rip off starving comedians

How book publishers rip off starving comedians

You have definately got this completely wrong - publishers rip NOBODY off.

We give everyone a really good deal, very fair indeed

*

Oh. Is it a joke? Ah yes, ha, ha, ha, ha, ha - Nice one Jasp!!

The Two Wallies - a lacerating sketch based on The Two

Ronnies - only starring Dr David Owen and David Steel

??? We rather like the SDP. Couldn't you make this a bit less political?

*

Great Virgins in History - by Barbara Cartland

*

Sorry Jasp- Barb's one of our authors! Jeffry Archer maybe ???

I've got this mole...

Spies? The whole spying thing is V. sensitive at present.

*

How Mikhael Gorbachev got that funny purple patch on his

head

Fine. But do we want to rock the boat just when the disarmament thing is getting going?

*

The day I tried to join the Freemasons

The chairman says drop this one if you value your kneecaps!

*

Esther Rantzen !!!

20 Things You Didn't Know about ~~Princess Michael of Kent~~

*

Carrott takes over ICI — *Yeah fine, but could we make it Distillers? the chairman's wife has a fair no of shares in I.C.I .!!*

*

Why I hate computers — *Doubtful about This. We do have a list of computer books you know. Typewriters? Televisions?*

CENSORED SCENES FROM MY AUTOBIOGRAPHY
MY PART IN THE PROFUMO SCANDAL

ow many people, I wonder, can claim to have brought down an entire government before they were out of their teens? Can count among their formative adolescent influences such notorious names as Lord X, Mr Y. MP, Viscount Z and Madame Tania Hide 'the Queen of Swish'? Can look back fondly on intimate, early experiences not of the pimply, grope-in-the-dark kind but on scenes of immense sophistication and originality, featuring (in no particular order) Lord Astor's housemaid, a well-known film actress, a fox terrier and Miss Mandy Rice-Davies?

Yes, it's true. I was the mysterious 'Mr C' in the great scandal of '62.

It all started one balmy September evening. The phone rang. My mother answered it.

'Harold Macmillan for you,' she said.

I picked up the receiver, my heart beating like the boom of shotguns on a Scottish grouse moor.

'Is that you, young Turnip?' said the familiar voice at the other end. Its frail, yet oddly warm tone was redolent with centuries of aristocratic in-breeding, golden retrievers, plus fours, trout streams, blazing log fires, fresh December afternoons riding to hounds, charades with members of the Royal Family, coming-out balls, risqué weekends in Paris at famous houses of ill repute, baronial mansions, grovelling butlers, blushing young servant-girls eager to –

'Are you there, Turnip?' A sharpness, an anger even, had entered the voice.

'C-Carrott, sir,' I stuttered.

'Mmm? Yes, yes, Carrott if you like. You do impressions, I hear. Duke of Edinburgh, me, John Wayne, that sort of game?'

'It's just a bit of fun, sir – '

'Shut up, Carrott! Can you do Profumo?'

Who the hell was Profumo?

'Course I can, sir,' I said quickly.

'Right. Grab yourself a hansom cab and get down to Downing Street sharpish. Your country needs you.'

Within moments, I had packed an overnight bag and was on my way to London – for the greatest adventure of my young life . . .

It's difficult to remember just how straight-laced Great Britain was in those dark and distant days. The Permissive Society had yet to be invented. Ken Tynan had yet to shock the nation by saying 'Poo' on BBC television. Herman's Hermits had yet to record their notorious hit 'I Want To Do Some Heavy Petting With You'. Lady Douglas-Withers had yet to make her famous defense in the House of Lords of permissiveness, the so-called 'I am wearing no knickers' speech'. And Roger Miller had yet to release what was to become the anthem of the let-it-all-hang-out generation, 'England Swings'.

For most of us youngsters, sex was a distant and dreaded prospect, something embarrassing and slightly messy that occasionally happened after lights out. The pill had been invented and I had used it for six months just in case. Then I found out you had to take it orally.

So imagine my confusion when Sir Harold Macmillan told me what I was expected to do on behalf of my country.

It was daring. It was dangerous. And it was pretty bloody filthy . . .

'Jack Profumo to see Lord Astor,' I announced at the massive, wrought-iron gates to his baronial home, Cliveden House.

'Password?' snarled the doorman suspiciously.

'Well he would, wouldn't he,' I said without a moment's hesitation.

MI5 had done their work well. The gates creaked open and the doorman pointed me the way to the house. Only then did I notice that he was wearing no trousers.

It was the first of many strange things I was to see at Cliveden that day.

There was no reply from the front door, so I made my way to the back of the house where a swimming-pool party was in full swing.

I shall never forget the sight that greeted me there. It was not the leather-clad butlers that shocked me, nor even the judge who was starkers except for his wig, nor the waitresses dressed up as schoolgirls, nor the well-known politician gambolling in the shallow end with Christine Keeler, nor the obstetrician Stephen Ward oiling the back of Brian Epstein as a stable lad read a Virginia Woolf short story to them.

What astounded and horrified me was that my prey, the Russian intelligence plant Ivanov was *not* joining in but was actually taking photographs of the party.

'Da, a little closer to her, Lord X,' he was chortling. 'Cheese, Mr Y – end smeck, smeck, smeck on the botty, Lord Z – da, da – great snaps for the family album!'

Standing there, I remembered Supermac's last words to me. 'If we can catch Ivanov getting his jollies with a couple of highly unsuitable young totties, then we'll have Mr Russkie where we want him. The Cold War will be over before you can say 'KGB MAN NABBED IN SHOCK VICE ORGY'. Go to it, Turnip!'

It was gin and tonic time at Cliveden. There was an air of post-coital languor about the place. The judge was picking the pubic hairs from his wig. The girls had left to freshen up for the evening, while Ward and Epstein had given up on Virginia Woolf and were taking a walk together in the woods.

I wandered over to where Ivanov was counting and labelling his films.

'Care for a game of strip backgammon?' I enquired casually.

'And vy does the Minister of War suddenly fancy a kids' game ven he has been playing the gooseberry all afternoon?'

'I thought it might be . . . fun.'

It was a long game and the sun was setting before I got Ivanov down to his underpants. Then, right on cue, Christine Keeler wandered on to the scene.

'Take over from me,' I said. 'I want to go and join the orgy in the stables.'

When I returned a few moments later, they were both naked. Wasting no time, I shot off some twenty snaps from the camera hidden in my codpiece. My mission accomplished, I slipped away before any of the so-called Cliveden Set realized that the course of history had been changed . . .

'You bungling, incompetent idiot, Turnip!'

We were in the Cabinet Room, accompanied only by the heads of MI5, MI6 and the Armed Forces. Lady Dorothy had been told that her presence would not be required on this occasion.

'But Supermac – ' I remonstrated. 'I got the pictures, didn't I? Ivanov in the buff with a highly unsuitable young totty. What more did you want?'

'Show him, Bertie,' said Supermac wearily.

The head of MI5 pushed some photographs across the desk. They were similar to the ones I had taken, but taken from the other side of the backgammon table. Ivanov and Christine Keeler were there, nakedly absorbed in their game. But there in the background stood somebody else, also scantily clad. He had a rapt look of concentration on his face as he watched what was going on in front of him. And there was a noticeable bulge in his codpiece.

'It was the camera, sir!' I protested.

'*I* know it was the camera,' said Supermac, '*you* know it was the camera. But how the hell are we going to explain to the *News of the World* it was the camera . . .?'

The rest is history. The scandal, the shame, the humiliation, the eventual downfall of the Tory government.

There were many theories as to why, after years of being governed by nicely spoken chaps with wing collars and houses in the country, we should suddenly in 1964 be landed with a pipe-smoking little nobody like Wilson.

Some said it was the result of thirteen years of Tory misrule.

Others said that the moment for the white heat of Labour's technological revolution had arrived.

Only a handful of people knew what the real cause for the collapse of civilized government in 1964 was.

Me and my bulky equipment.

Some years later, I was to hear from my friends in MI5 once again. This time, they wanted me to go to Australia, leave my clothes on a beach and disappear. Had to call myself something like Stonehouse, if I remember rightly.

But that's another story . . .

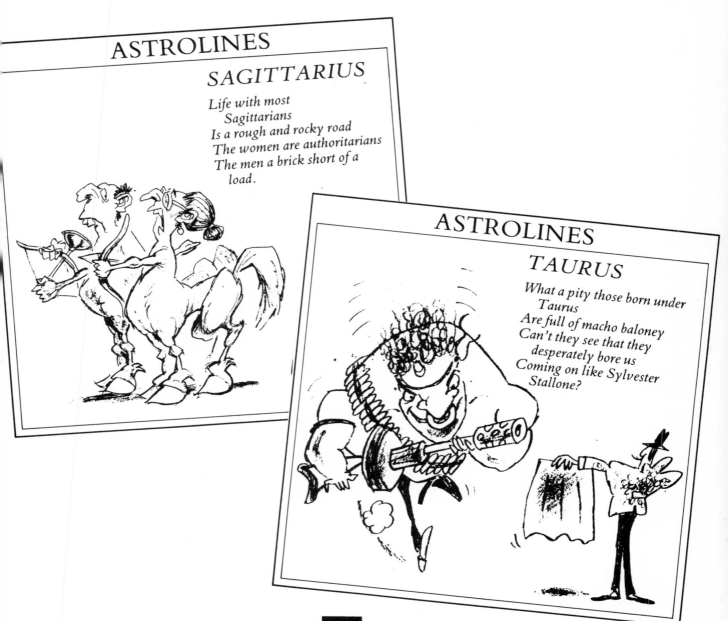

ASTROLINES

SAGITTARIUS

Life with most
Sagittarians
Is a rough and rocky road
The women are authoritarians
The men a brick short of a
load.

ASTROLINES

TAURUS

What a pity those born under
Taurus
Are full of macho baloney
Can't they see that they
desperately bore us
Coming on like Sylvester
Stallone?

THE Sun
Readers' TRIVIAL PURSUIT

Announcing the ULTIMATE family game for those with the attention span of an invertebrate!

Now try these questions

★ In the sensational *Sun* sexclusive 'STREET STAR IN THREE-IN-BED LOVE TANGLE', how many people were involved?

★ Who wrote Joan Collins' auto-biography?

★ Which end of the cue do you hit a snooker ball with?

★ On which page of your soaraway *Sun* does busty lovely Samantha Fox most frequently appear?

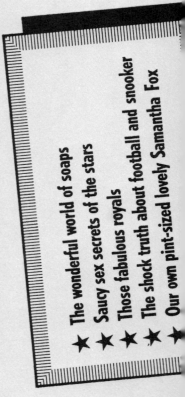

★ Krauts, frogs, nips, argies and dagos are types of what?

★ Did Britain's Prime Minister win the last G...

Yes it's true

After literally millions of hours of research involving three tons of mogadon, an in-depth interview with Russell Grant, a short, thick plank and a team of reasonably intelligent orang utangs, we've managed to drag Trivial Pursuit down to the intellectual level of the average Sun reader.

Do you know anything at all about the following:

★ The wonderful world of soaps
★ Saucy sex secrets of the stars
★ Those fabulous royals
★ The shock truth about football and snooker
★ Our own pint-sized lovely Samantha Fox

That's right, folks, this one's for you. Here are some posers which even the editor of the *Sun* could answer without first checking with his secretary (flame-haired cutie Amanda, aged eighteen, from Luton.)

★ Does the character 'Dirty Den' appear in Call My Bluff, EastEnders or Panorama?

★ Which famous female American pop star is named after the Virgin Mary?

Well, *Sun* readers, your brains must be hurting after all that — so here's something to 'pick you up'!

JO IS BUSTIN' OUT ALL OVER!

In our never-ending quest for younger and younger Page 3 girls, we've come up with a real treat for you lucky fellers! Lovely, bouncy brunette Jo Philips was only born in January but, thanks to her exceptionally greedy parents, we've managed to get her stripped down to her bare essentials in double-quick time. 'Goo-goo goo poo,' quipped saucy Jo when we told her she was Miss Sun Readers' Trivial Pursuit – and we don't think she was making an editorial comment. Cheeky!

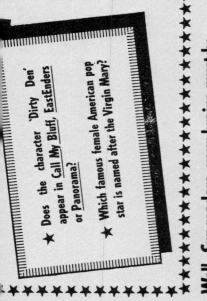

BETTER?????....

YES!!! I am an incredibly thick *Sun* reader and would like to be sent FREE for a mere £19.99 a set of the fabulous NEW game SUN READERS' TRIVIAL PURSUIT.

My average IQ is this many. ☜

THUMB-PRINT:

NAME: ....

ADDRESS: ....

(Crosses will not be acceptable.)

Great, then you'll be ready to fill in the form. (If you have difficulty working out which end of the pen to use, then get a neighbour to help.)

THE FREEZER

uring the very cold winter of early '86 the extreme temperatures affected every mechanical, energy-reliant household appliance in the home. Except one – the deep-freeze refrigerator cabinet. While fan heaters frizzled to a halt and TV sets blinked monotonously in sullen silence, the good old chest freezer burbled on merrily. The one item in the whole of the house that could have broken down in the adverse conditions and not one jot be given was simply glowing with health.

There is something extremely irksome surveying damn great lumps of ice blocking up the view from the garage and seeing the same substance staring at you from the inside of a freezer and knowing it's costing you money to keep it that way. What is more annoying is the sure-fire knowledge that some poor geezer in the middle of the tropics is up to his eyeballs in sweat trying to repair the identical model.

I did try as an experiment to sabotage this particular fridge. Against the maker's specific instructions, I chipped away the large lumps of ice that had formed around the interior. I used a large, uneven chisel and a 10-lb lump hammer. The ice was very thick and a mite difficult to remove. After about an hour I gave the Bird's Eye company a ring to see if they wanted to buy some pack ice. There were large dents inflicted onto the plastic interior and some quite severe scars too, but the motor if anything seemed to be quieter. But then anything seemed to be quiet after ceasing to use that lump hammer.

Having proved my theory I wondered how best to use this indestructible period of the freezer's existence, because as sure as 'eggs is eggs' come the summer it would break down. Firstly, it was very useful to use the three-pin plug attached to the freezer to test for dud fuses from other plugs where the appliances did not work. Secondly I could run a permanent lead from the motor of the freezer to the defunct fan heater. A brilliant idea, that is, if you have no electrical engineering knowledge whatsoever. If you do, you will know that it does not work. On the other hand, you can certainly keep warm from the ensuing fire and the heat conveniently melts the pack ice.

I now have to admit that I ran out of ideas of how to use the indefatigable freezer, but did note one or two other points of interest.

Firstly having emptied the cabinet of frozen goods I was surprised to see items of food at the bottom I had forgotten were ever made. They had been there some time it's true – this could be determined by the two shillings and sixpence price tag or the one and eleven pence reduced from nine shillings sales flash.

Did you know that before fish fingers you could buy cod balls? Or how about frozen liquid spam or puréed lamb and swede with added fat.

When I come to think of it fat was good for you twenty years ago. Manufacturers went to great lengths to inform you of the product's fat content. Lashings of fat, great globules of pulsating cellulose in every tin. 'Look at Eskimoes,' they urged, they survive in sixty degrees of frost on whale blubber – surely fat will see you through our English summers.

Fibre, of course, was totally unheard of. In fact, manufacturers took great pains to sieve any trace of the stuff out of the food. The theory was that fibre was so bulky it stopped you cramming great gobsful of processed food into your intestines, which in turn affected profits, and so out it went.

Additives too were proudly proclaimed on the front of packets. Some products had so much preservative they claimed a shelf life that would take them well into the next century. Pests like rats, ants and bacteria had more sense than to go anywhere near them and had quite a hard time surviving in the early seventies.

Sugar too was then an energy source, not the poison it's regarded as now. Sugar was right up there with the new discovery, vitamins. Not too many vitamins, mind – got to make way for the sugar! Any food without sugar was almost shunned by the public, they wanted sugar in *everything*. The Egg Marketing Board (remember 'Go to work on an egg'?) were even considering injecting eggs with it. Nowadays, of course, sugar is discreetly labelled somewhere in the back corner and called fructose or lactose or glucose to hide the true amount the product contains. The taste buds still crave the flavour, it's just that we don't want to admit we are eating it.

Among other foods seeing daylight for the first time in two decades were a suet pudding, a Dan Dare ice lolly and, sad to say, Hercules the hamster who went missing two days after Christmas 1971. Still, he was perfectly preserved and we gave him a little private burial.

The other interesting point was we couldn't get all the goods we had emptied out back into the freezer. Could it be because matter expands at a higher temperature? Well yes, but it was five degrees colder outside than in. I decided to leave the extra goods outside overnight to ponder the problem, and anyway the pubs were open and I could get some advice from the regulars.

Next morning the sun was shining, and as I walked into the garden there was a pile of soggy food outside the garage in the middle of which was the dog chewing the remains of the cod balls.

LIVING WITH THE CURSE

I would like to shed some light on an extremely embarrassing subject that we all know about but rarely discuss except in sheltered nooks and whispered conversations.

I'm talking about that regular body cycle that only a certain human gender suffer from. It makes them extremely volatile and unpredictable; their physical features change and there's quite a lot of blood involved. Well, we are all adults except for children so let's name names. What I'm referring to is facial hair – man's curse.

How would women like it if every morning they woke up to find this black hedging growing out of their chins and cheeks? What facial hair women *do* get sends them AWOL. Eyebrows which are pretty normal, inoffensive facial features – unless you're Dennis Healey – cause certain women to act in a most puzzling tribal manner. They spend hours in front of a bathroom mirror painfully plucking every single hair from their eyebrows. Having achieved this Kojak state of appearance they then grab a big black lump of crayon and fill it all back in again.

Now just imagine the problem men have having to deal with this problem on a much larger scale every day. It would help if women could make a note in their diaries of when the more problematical times are likely to occur. A particularly susceptible time is early in the morning. This is when the curse usually raises its ugly head and action has to be taken right away.

Men are very touchy in this situation. Help them. Make sure the water is the right temperature, shake the aerosol shaving cream sufficiently so it will produce a nice foamy lather, and he will really appreciate that warm, dry towel ready and waiting to pat his face nice and dry. A useful tip here; I always carry a spare pack of Gillette II in a plain paper bag just in case I get caught in a restaurant or something.

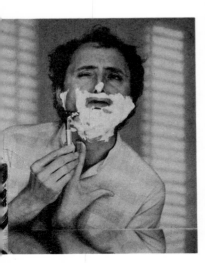

I wish more research could be done on PST – Pre Shaving Tension. Most of the so-called accidents when shaving could be avoided if only the true cause of them would be more recognized. I have a theory that large infusions of alcohol late at night have a related effect to PST the following morning. The residual, muscular spasms resulting in jerky, uncoordinated strokes of the razor blade can cause permanent disfiguration. As I say it's only a theory, but I'm involved with much empirical research at present and in time I'm sure my suspicions will be vindicated or eventually obliterated.

Another cause of PST is faulty alarm clocks. The fallibility of these imprecise instruments can be vouched for by many a works management, employee after employee arriving late for work because the alarm device was not activated in time sufficient to enable them to prepare for the day's labour ahead. PST is most prevalent at these moments of stress.

In the rush to avoid dereliction of duty, large chunks of facial carcass

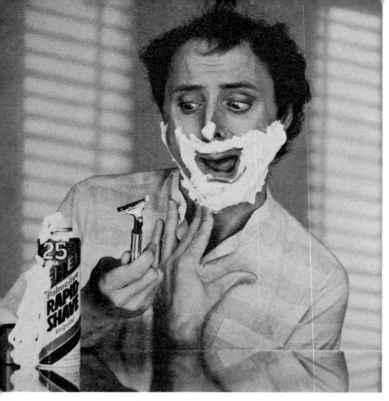

are removed almost unnoticed. Great gobsful of muesli ballooning out the cheeks don't help and the smooth, svelte action of the shaving cream is hindered substantially by mixing it with toasted breadcrumbs and marmalade.

Other causes of PST which could be investigated are Bathroom Children; maturing malevolents who live in bathrooms from 7.30 a.m. to 8.50 a.m. It would seem any exposure to stairs or landing areas between these times will produce instant death or something equivalent; it must do, it's the only explanation for their constant occupation of these rooms. It can't be too safe for them either in the bathroom.

At 8.50 a.m. they open the door and rush out frothing at the mouth like a demented mad dog. 'Oh! That's toothpaste,' I hear you mock in disbelief. Wrong! It can't be toothpaste because that's all over the floor and bidet and cistern and door handles and everywhere except in the tube. I reckon if ever they find an ointment to cure herpes they should put it in toothpaste tubes, give them all to children and there would be such a blanket coverage of ointment no herpes virus would stand an earthly.

The sight of all this smeared toothpaste in the bathroom is, when I come to think about it, the main cause of PST. At about 23p a square centimetre the thought of the cost would make even the most spendthrift shaver gouge his face to pieces to make him appear as if he'd just dunked his face into a Magi-mix.

An attempt to alleviate the problems of man's curse came with the invention of the electric shaver. This appliance was meant to relieve the yoke of man's burden to impress the opposite sex. Not so. They don't work. Mainly because they are full of toothpaste. Even when they are de-Colgated the effectiveness is negligible. After twenty minutes of massaging the face, the resultant loss of hair is the same as if you'd used a hair dryer.

I will, no doubt, one day be asked by the *Lancet* to write some anthropological essay on this ill-discussed phenomena. I will then expound on such diverse aspects as why razor blades become so sharp after shaving hairs on legs they can slice unimpeded through throats.

And why if main arteries can be blocked and healed by layers of *Daily Mirror* applied with large globules of spittle, why does the National Health Service waste millions of pounds on needles and thread?

And finally, why don't Red Indians have beards or moustaches? Never in any cowboy and Indian film have I ever seen a redskin – be it Sioux or Cheyenne – sprouting a handlebar growth or a goatee protrusion. This can't all be put down to the lack of shaver points in tepees surely? That's why they went round scalping people so they could use the hair to go to

fancy dress parties dressed up like Toulouse Lautrec.

Here's a thought. Men that grow moustaches and beards are always thought to be hiding something, or they are insecure because of some unconfessed childhood trauma like mixing Shredded Wheat with grand-dad's pipe tobacco. It could be that this facial hair is to identify with the macho cowboy image, the winner, the man who always gets the girl. Subconsciously they have sussed the fact redskins can't grow the stuff. Which is why men who smoke pipes generally have beards as well. In their mind they are symbolic trophies from some raid on a savage Shawnee village.

My word, isn't life simple when you analyse it?

CARROTT'S LIFE

Jasper Carrot
C O M E D I A N

CARROTT'S
~~THIS IS YOUR LIFE~~

5 January

Dear Eamonn

I just wanted you to know that, after years of trying to avoid your programme, it finally caught up with me last night. I was just tuning into a 'World in Action' special on the problems of the Third World when - whammo there you were, all pearly teeth and Harry Fenton suit, victimizing some harmless little music-hall turn I'd never heard of - Mike someone was it? Little bloke with a cute smile and silly glasses anyway.

It occurred to me that if you're scraping the barrel for 'This Is Your Life' guests (who next, I wonder - Dirty Den? Patrick Jenkin? My cleaning lady?), you might take it into your head to go to the top and ask me to appear in a Special.

Well frankly, Eamonn, forget it. I'm not going to sit there looking totally stupid while all the people I manage to avoid except at Christmas troop in front of me for the benefit of millions of early-evening viewers.

So tell your researchers not to bother trying to set the whole thing up with my wife (office no: 654 2761) - we're simply not interested in that kind of showbiz ego-trip.

Yours

Jasper Carrott

Jasper Carrott

Jasper Carrot
C O M E D I A N

23 January

Dear Eamonn

I'm very surprised that you have seen fit to ignore my letter of 5 January and have failed to cancel plans for a 'This Is Your Life' spectacular starring myself. So much for showbiz solidarity!

Just to let you know how serious I am about this, here are some of the precautionary steps I'll be taking:

1. I'm not going anywhere near the Thames Television studios where you usually jump out and take the star celeb. by surprise, except for one Tuesday evening in March. (No, I'm <u>not</u> going to tell you which Tuesday - I'm not falling for that old trick!)

2. I've told my friend Tony Fisher, who lives in Melbourne, not to accept gifts of air-tickets to London from smooth-talking strangers. He's agreed, except for the third week of March when, for private, religious reasons, he's obliged to agree to all proposals put to him involving first-class travel by Qantas, with free champagne thrown in.

3. I've asked my children (they look great on television, Eamonn - what a pity you can't use them!) to take Tuesday 23 March off school so that the whole family can go to London on a family trip. This is to compensate for my not appearing on 'This Is Your Life' which, for reasons which escape me, is a bit of a disappointment to them.

4. I'm taking crying lessons from Sir Dickie Attenborough.
Don't know why I mentioned that. Just thought you might be
interested.

Please don't waste any more of my time. If you're really
desperate, what about Paul 'Not a lot' Daniels?

Your fellow Equity member

Jasper Carrott

Has anyone mentioned that you look like a wine waiter with
that ridiculous red book under your arm?

Jasper Carrot

C O M E D I A N

24 January

Dear Eamonn

If your researchers happen to turn up someone called Mademoiselle
Tania from Brewer Street, London W1, please ignore anything she
says about me. Between you and me, she'll really lower the tone
of the programme and then blab to the <u>Sunday People</u> about it.

Not that I've met her. I've just heard rumours.

Yours, man to man

Jasper Carrott
Jasper Carrott

P.S. It's not true what she says about the baby lotion and
the Joan Collins inflatable traffic warden.

P.P.S. And the dachshund was her idea.

Jasper Carrot

C O M E D I A N

9 February

Dear Eamonn

It appears that there is unfortunately nothing that I can do in law to prevent hoards of your overpaid staff combing through my private life for the delectation of the prurient, square-eyed divots who watch your ridiculous show.

So be it. But don't think I'm going to make it easy for you. My wife's cousins, who live in Utah, tell me that they will <u>not</u> come over unless it's on Concorde. Uncle Milt's a big man and, if you palm him off with a scheduled flight, I can't be answerable for the consequences.

I enclose a list of relations you should not under any circumstances invite, <u>even as members of the audience</u>. If I catch sight of so much as one mad or drunk cousin, I'll be out of the studio before you can say 'shillelagh'.

I'm told that my left side is best for the cameras, but I expect I'll have the chance to brief the cameramen, sound, lighting etc. as to my precise requirements. Leave it to the professionals, eh Eamonn?

Yours in anticipatio

Jasper

Jasper Carrott

Jasper Carrot

C O M E D I A N

10 March

Dear Eamonn

I like the way your people are getting on with the show without bothering me. Still, it's only a fortnight away now so maybe t like to do some kind of readthrough with me.

I'd like some feedback re my bursting into tears bit. For instance, is it best for me to break down when you first take me by surprise, when you talk about my first break into television or while I'm being mobbed by friends and fans as the closing credits roll? Perhaps the director can count me down on the night - thanks to Sir Dickie's help, I can be in floods in a matter of seconds.

A minor point from my legal people. Please bill the programme as 'This Is CARROTT'S Life'. Otherwise we walk away from the who deal.

Jasper Carrot
C O M E D I A N

Wednesday 24 March

Dear Eamonn

Where were you?

That is the last – and I mean the <u>last</u> – time I agree to do anything to help the ratings of your pathetic apology for a show.

Last night I spent three hours – <u>three hours</u>, Eamonn – in the Thames Television VIP car park, wandering around as if nothing's going to happen. And what happens? Nothing.

D'you think I <u>like</u> getting into my make-up and stage gear to stand around in the freezing cold, trying to look casual. And how d'you think I looked in front of my entire family who were waiting expectantly in a hired coach just round the corner. Uncle Milt wasn't impressed either, after his long trip from Utah.

I enclose my bill – well I warned you Milt's family had to fly Concorde – and would ask you never ever to bother me again.

If you want to make things up with me, you can tell your fellow blarney-merchant Wogan that I am <u>not</u> available for interviews – particularly during the last week of next month.

Yours

Jasper Carrott

Jasper Carrott

A ROUND WITH MAX

I call him affectionately the curly-headed garden gnome, he calls me the poor man's Max Boyce. Both quotes are, needless to say, from newspapers. Max Boyce is that Welsh enigma that no one has yet explained or is ever likely to. Over the years we have become good friends and I'm indebted to him many times for his unlimited kindness and generosity. We don't see each other that often and in the nicest possible way it's probably just as well.

An evening spent in the company of Max would test the staying power of Frank Bruno and the constitution of Oliver Reed.

The first couple of times we got together were firstly in Swansea and then in Cardiff. That much I remember, the rest is sort of familiar confirmed by other inebriated eye witnesses and statements from my manager and casual observers.

Our inaugural meeting took place in a small restaurant in South Wales. I had just finished a show in one of those sport leisure centres, large cavernous halls that are converted for the odd night into a London Palladium. Apart from being about as intimate as a DHSS waiting room, the sound problems can be horrendous. This particular one had an echo that would have shamed a Swiss ski resort, in fact, if you went back today you could probably still hear the same show going on and on and on.

Max had just returned from officiating at some local charity-sponsored privet hedge-clipping or whatever and the evening began.

Something we both share in common is the fact that we both still live in the communities we grew up in. The opportunity to talk to somebody in the same boat about 'the biz' was irresistible. We talked about our deep love for the press, and how difficult it is spending £4 million pounds a year on yourself because no one understands. The pressures of the road, and doesn't BBC make-up so dry the skin.

At that time Max had a passion for a white wine called Pouilly Foussé, a cheeky, impertinent little nectar that he had become quite fond of – well, obsessed would be more like it. He insisted that I cultivate the obsession too.

We left the restaurant at about 1 a.m., the table was in that sort of state that looks as if the food has been eaten through the tablecloth. Arm in arm, professing undying friendship, we went in search of 'more of that porky, incontinent little chappy Filly Puss'.

Swansea at 1.30 a.m. does not abound with chintzy little wine bars prepared to serve two extremely noisy gentlemen with crates of 'fussy smelly Chocky Piss'.

It was the misfortune of the Dragon Hotel in Swansea to have reserved me a room. This of course meant that I was a resident and therefore eligible to demand a drink at whatever hour of the day or night. The night porter was summoned and asked to supply a vat of 'Fully Fused Frilly

Froth'. My manager, who was on hand and sober through all this and resigning himself to a night of picking up the bits, translated our request to the night porter. The porter was in a state of agitation. Before him was not a curly-headed garden gnome but Max Boyce, a Welsh Deity! A very loud and wobbly deity, true, but nonetheless a Welsh one. He didn't have any Frilly Froth but he *did* have the next best thing – Harp lager.

This regrettable state of affairs took some time to explain during which Max's concentration lapsed and he began to replay the events leading up to a very famous Welsh try against the New Zealanders with the help of the porter's hat. The chandeliers were the goalposts and the armchair was a famous Kiwi full-back called Bonehead. Max was Gazza Edwards. Gazza ran off down the corridor sidestepping the entire New Zealand rugby team twice only to come hurtling back into the lobby full-tilt into Bonehead. Having scored the try he then proceeded to place kick the porter's cap between the chandeliers.

The porter walked hesitantly away to retrieve his cap and off to the bar to supply the lager. He was obviously puzzled. Deities, Welsh or not, don't go round punting porters' hats through chandeliers. While he was away I took the opportunity to remind Max of how Geoff Hurst scored his hat-trick against the Germans in 1966. True, I didn't have the porter's hat, but a cushion nestling in the corner of the armchair wasn't a bad substitute.

We retired to the lounge to partake of the Harp lager supplied by a now very anxious porter. I'm ashamed to say but from here on in the evening got out of hand. I can't for the life of me remember what we did, but at 4 a.m. my manager was on the phone trying to contact any world stockmarket that was open and attempting to purchase Harp lager shares.

Max had assembled all the lounge furniture by now to represent the entire New Zealand scrum pack. I was perched on top of this yelling to the imaginary 60,000 people at Cardiff Arms Park to sing a rather rude version of 'Wild Rover'.

We were violently loud – so loud a group of nine very drunken sales reps in the bar next door came in and requested a reduction in volume as they were trying to sing rugby songs.

However, Max was in full flight. He preceded Rambo by at least five years; he got, if anything, louder and the New Zealand scrum pack was now up to the ceiling. My manager and I then witnessed one of the bravest moments in Welsh history. The porter entered the lounge, walked up to Max and said that if he didn't stop the noise he would have to leave the hotel! This monumental display of raw courage impressed even my addled brain. Can you imagine some Vatican guard walking up to the Pope in St Peter's Square and saying, 'Look, either stop all this blessing, mate, or sling yer hook!' Now if ever I own a hotel, that's the porter I'd want guarding it.

Max, confronted with this threat, actually stopped in mid scrum, took one look at the porter and immediately co-opted him on to the front row.

For me it was time to retire. That little voice inside the head that says 'enough is enough' was insisting that I went to bed. I took a look around the lounge. It was like the end of the first day's sale at MFI. In one of those futile gestures that inebriated people make, I tried to put an ashtray back in the middle of a table so's the cleaning lady wouldn't have much to do the next morning. But it had to be *exactly* in the middle. My manager enticed me into the lift by explaining there was a slide rule in the bedroom and I could use that to check the ashtray's central position. As I left the lounge my final observation was that of a porter trying to assert his authority which is difficult when you're wearing a very, very bent hat, over a demented curly-headed garden gnome clambering up a great pile of furniture.

We met several times after that, once in a Chinese restaurant in Cardiff and once at a celebrity ball in Birmingham. We are told that each time we went through exactly the same conversation as the first time we met. It was obvious to the pair of us that we were bad news for each other and we made a pact that next time we met it would be sensible. HAH!

Around about the early eighties Max and I had taken up the game of golf, independently I have to admit. For me it was a somewhat humiliating experience. For years I had been ridiculing the game and anyone who played it. It was an old man's game, about as interesting as a Morris Marina and definitely sniggersville. Fatally, I accepted an invitation from a friend to try a round of golf. With my 'sack of bats' (snigger) and an air of superiority I went round nine holes in well over a hundred strokes doing a very fair impression of a one-legged drain. Convinced that it was just a case of mind over matter, after all the ball is not *moving*, it's stock still, there's no reaction to it – just do the same thing over and over again and it's all down to who can be luckiest at putting. And so like millions of others, I got hooked on the most infuriating, pointless, rule-ridden game in existence, and never enjoyed anything so much in all of my sporting life.

Max was also smitten at about the same time and so we agreed to play a head-to-head at a mutually convenient course between Swansea and Birmingham. This turned out to be St Pierre Golf and Country Club near Chepstow.

The club professional was Brian Hugget, an ex-Ryder Cup player and general 'good egg'. He made us very welcome with free trees, a golf ball without the name crossed out and even went so far as to loan us an electric rolley which he assured us would speed up our play. We placed both sets of clubs into the trolley and made our way to the first tee. We were both playing off a handicap of 21, no great shakes but it was early days and in six months' time each one of us was reasonably confident that the likes of Nick Faldo, Sandy Lyle, etc. would be quaking in their plus fours.

It was a bright, warm June day and we hadn't had any rain for quite a while so conditions were perfect. Taking our drivers from our bags we started a few practice swings, swooshing and swashing and looking very professional. I went off first and gave the ball quite a reasonable thwack, unfortunately so far left it went on to the adjacent fairway. Max walked up and did exactly the same thing, except to the right.

We set off in the trolley first to Max's ball whereupon he got out, set up and knocked it further to the right. He got back into the trolley and we hared across the fairway through some trees to my ball on the adjacent fairway on the left. I got out, set up and hit it out to the left, not as far as Max had hit his so we got back into the trolley and drove straight to mine. I hit the next shot somewhere in the vicinity of the green and then it was into the trolley to hare back to the trees across the fairway over to Max's ball on the right. This went on for six or seven holes. If we had been carrying our own bags it would have been the most unsociable game of golf ever recorded. Instead we were inseparable; back and forth across the fairways and rough in this glorified milk float. I honestly wondered if there was enough charge in the battery to get us round the whole eighteen holes, and did this thing have headlights? Because at this rate we were going to need them.

I have to report (it's my book so no one's going to stop me) that on approaching the eighth tee I was seven holes up. I had won every one much to Max's chagrin. I wish I could report that I had been playing well. This was not the case. Max was having a 'mare'. He was consistently hitting the ball out to the left with a banana-like trajectory that is commonly called 'a slice'. And a very nasty slice it was too. Somewhere about the fifth tee I thought I would lighten the occasion with a jocular remark. Standing well behind Max, who was just about to cream a 4-iron, I said, 'Don't worry Max, I'll catch this one!' He got into the cart and drove off without me.

My shot off the eighth tee was pretty good; just off the fairway and a good 250 yards down wind. Max, whipping off the cover of his driver, teeth clenched, informed me he had had enough of this messing about and that this ball was going to be propelled several million miles away, and when it arrived it would be minus its dimples. He did indeed give it one hell of a larruping. It screamed off at the speed of light only fractionally off course. Just enough off course to strike the middle of a large tree. The ball sailed back over our heads to land fifty yards behind us.

One of the unwritten rules of golf (no doubt it will soon be included) is that you are not allowed to guffaw at your opponent's misfortune. I didn't guffaw, nearly – but I didn't. Max was pretty uppity about that last shot. He walked the fifty yards back to his ball, still with his driver in his hand and squared up to give the ball another similar blow. Hitting a ball with a driver off the deck, i.e., no tee peg, is rarely attempted even by the likes of

Jack Nicklaus. It is a very difficult shot to execute and much to Max's credit, after reading the last rites to his Dunlop '65, he hit one of the best shots I've seen from a 21-handicapper, ever. I'm sure it would have gone 400 yards minimum. It was stopped from achieving this momentous length by the self-same tree that inhibited the previous shot. It didn't quite hit the middle this time, in fact, it came off at about an angle of 30 degrees. After ricocheting off several other types of timber it finally flew back and nestled at the edge of the fairway some five yards ahead of Max.

Unwritten rule or no unwritten rule I did shriek with uncontrolled mirth, I did roll over and over, I did clutch my sides and I did bend double pounding the earth with my fists. I apologized profusely but I don't think Max was too convinced. Six shots later he reached the green; not that I would have performed much better if I'd had someone behind me constantly guffawing every time I hit the ball.

Coming off the ninth green I was eight holes up. We made our way across to the tenth tee to start the final nine holes.

On the way we had to pass close to the professionals' shop where we saw Mr Hugget checking his watch in disbelief at the time we were taking. We gave him a cheerful wave as we went past and did a figure of eight in the cart to show him we had mastered the steering and controls. He retreated back into his shop with much muttering and shaking of the head.

The next six holes were relatively uneventful, but on the 16th hole a minor mishap occurred. I had won the match by this stage and we were playing the rest of the holes for a £1 bet. Not a pools' win I agree, but there was more than a pound at stake here, this was England v. Wales!

I drove off the 16th tee into some trees on the right. The next shot was going to be difficult but not impossible. Max teed his ball up, and in attempting to hit it into the Irish Sea squirted his ball straight left ten yards into a ditch which was at the bottom of a small copse. He impatiently declared the ball lost and was about to reload on the tee when I said, 'Hold on Max, at least look for the ball. I'm in trouble, if you find yours you might have a lucky break and be able to play it.'

I found Max's ball halfway up the side of the rather steep ditch. It was nestled nicely in the middle of a clump of grass, not the easiest shot in the world but eminently playable. Max was all for picking it up and playing again off the tee, a penalty of two shots. 'Now look, Max,' I insisted, 'take your sand wedge and play the ball out on to the fairway, two more shots and a putt and you're down for five.'

Common sense won the day and he stepped down into the ditch and squared up to the ball with his sand wedge. As I mentioned earlier it was a bright warm day, in fact rain hadn't been seen for several weeks, courses all over Britain were hard and dry and both of us were wearing the appropriate, smart, light-coloured slacks and 'Medallion Man' top shirts with the little alligator on. Very swish.

As Max's sand wedge descended I was fortunate to be standing many yards away because as he hit the ball the club followed through into the bottom of the bank and hit the only patch of wet earth in the whole of Gwent. And very wet it was too. It sprayed up into the air with a terrific mount of velocity because not only was Max trying to get the ball on to the fairway, he was attempting to reach the green. He was smack in the middle of the vortex, and emerged from the ditch with a most impressive array of decorum covered in such an amount of mud that the alligator looked quite at home.

My decorum did not match his. I laughed extremely loudly. I also asked him if he could impersonate Al Jolson. Back into the golf cart and off to finish the 16th and 17th holes. I was still chuckling as we approached the 18th and final hole. If we both knew what was going to happen we would have gone home there and then.

The finishing hole at St Pierre is very well known and very well respected amongst the golfing fraternity. It is a very long 240-yard par-3 that stretches slightly uphill towards the club house. Between tee and green there is a formidable and foreboding lake that sucks in golf balls like some giant goldfish. It is approached with trepidation at the best of times. On this occasion it was even more nerve-racking because of the sight that greeted our eyes. The clubhouse at the back of the green has a large balcony halfway up that gives a superb view of the complete hole. The rumour had gone round that Max and I were on the course and were due to finish any time in the next four hours. Being late afternoon people who had stopped in for a drink on the way home, golfers who had already finished and other general oddbods had gathered on the balcony curious to see how two comedians played golf. They were not to be disappointed.

As I placed my ball on a tee and lined up the shot I could not help but see the enormous crowd gathered on the balcony. The wind was blowing into our faces not only making the shot more difficult but also carrying the noise of the spectators down wind. I knew I had no chance of reaching the green so I was just concentrating and praying, 'Please God, don't let me put one in the drink.' My prayers were answered and the ball sailed over the lake only to fade into the heavy rough on the right-hand side. As it landed we heard mild, ironic applause from the gallery. I thought I'll settle for that on this occasion.

Max was in a dilemma; take an easy five-iron and clear the lake for safety or go for broke with the driver. You can't keep a good showman down. Here was an audience to impress. Out came the driver, ball on tee, almighty swing, ball hit so high it came down with ice on it just far enough to clear the lake by inches and into some bushes and clag way over to the left. The cheers from the balcony were loud but good-natured.

We piled into the golf cart and drove down what we thought was the golf cart track. Halfway down we realized it wasn't. I thought it was a bit steep as we started but as the track narrowed it also got steeper. The left-hand wheels were now over the edge of a very steep bank, and the cart was in serious danger of toppling over. There was no alternative but to get out and manoeuvre the whole damn wretched thing by hand down the rest of the track. While Max supported the left-hand side to stop it falling sideways I was up front full weight against the thing to stop it careering downhill and into the lake. Believe me, those carts are some weight, and it took us a full ten minutes to heave and hump the vehicle down to the bottom. This was manna from heaven to the assembled crowd which had doubled and was now heaving on the balcony. During our efforts faint pieces of advice came floating down wind – 'Put your backs into it' and 'Hit it with your driver' – and they were as unwelcome as they were unfunny.

We drove to Max's ball. He could just about play it. Straddled over a large tree stump, his view obscured by overhanging trees, he miraculously got the ball out into play. I left him with a seven-iron to get to the green then dashed into the cart to play my shot. As I got out of the cart to play my ball Max was shouting to me, 'Jasper, Jasper, bring me my sand wedge.'

'What?'

'Bring me my sand wedge, I've knocked it back into the clag.'

He had hit his seven-iron, and the ball had hit the wall that ran up the left-hand side of the course and had indeed ran back into the clag. I dashed back in the cart with his sand wedge then back across to my ball. Watched by a crowd now expecting anything to happen I prepared to hit a high floating wedge shot over the sand bunker and on to the green. I took the wedge back slowly and with majestic rhythm and accuracy brought the clubface into contact with the ball. It travelled precisely three inches. The clapping and cheering were beginning to get on my nerves.

I took aim again, and this time connected a little better only to see the ball land in the bunker on the right-hand side of the green. More cheers. Now it was Max's turn. Having got his ball out of the clag he hit his seven-iron again and the ball, true to form, flew up in the air over the wall and out of bounds. The crowd were now in a very silly mood. I forget most of the comments but the one that really stood out was, 'As golfers you make bloody good comedians.'

The agony was still not over. While we were admittedly furkling around, a team of four ladies had been waiting patiently on the 18th tee for us to finish. We knew this because we were informed of it in the most embarrassing way possible. A club official, some big-time nobody whose greatest claim to fame was that he scored a hole in seven on a par-three, came galumphing out of the club house. He was a strange, bespectacled little man who looked like Magnus Pyke only more animated. Determined to make a name for himself and uphold the sacred rules of golf he started screaming at me, 'Let them through, let them through.'

There is a rule in golf that says if you are holding players up let them pass you so they can get on with their game. I am aware of the rule more than most, but as it was the final hole I thought that was taking courtesy to the extreme and I told him so. The glare he gave me welded his glasses to his nose. I relented and called the ladies through.

I sat dejectedly in the cart. The ladies played the hole in abnormally quick time and as they left the green the most embarrassing experience in my whole golfing career to date took place.

Max had hit his golf ball out of bounds and the rules of golf say that you must pick the ball up or go back and play another ball from the same spot where you had played the last shot. Max was unaware of this rule. To help facilitate the finding of lost balls out of bounds and to stop golfers clambering up and over the wall a door had been placed in the wall

opposite the green. Now not only had Max found his ball in the out-of-bounds area, he was committing a cardinal golfing sin by attempting to play it while out of bounds, and not just playing it. Oh no! Not Max. The ball was only two feet from the wall so there was no chance of hitting the ball up and over. The crowd watched in disbelief – then disbelief turned into incredulity as Max calmly walked to the door and started to angle it so that he could hit the ball off the door and on to the green.

Jigger me, he went and did it! As the ball clunked off the door and rolled on to the green the spectators went bananas. It was reported that some actually fell off the balcony. With as much dignity as possible we putted out, shook hands and climbed into the cart. There was just enough electricity to drive the twenty yards to the pro shop and hand over to Mr Hugget. With clapping and cheering in our ears we slunk off to the back bar to evaluate our performance and draw lots as to who could tell the story of the day's events first. I won.

ASTROLINES

LIBRA

Librans are rarely excited
So passive, shy and demure
That in a library, Librans are
    liable
To appear silent, calm and
    obscure.

The

Jasper Carrott

WINE

SUPPLEMENT

KNOW YOUR WINES

A SAMPLER'S GUIDE

SPANISH VINE GARO

Strong, simple and frequently lethal, this wine is sometimes known as the 'Rambo of the vineyard'.

FRENCH VIN TRÈS ORDINAIRE

Our picture shows this popular vin de table being enjoyed by French wine-lovers at the famous Lyons wine festival.

GERMAN UTTERGNATSPISSEN

The high price of this shocking little wine is said to be caused by the cost of capturing it in millions of small latrine buckets in the heart of the Black Forest.

TASMANIAN DINGO VALLEY BAR RAG

Containing subtle hints of sawdust, Fosters lager, dog's mess and the barman's chew-baccy, this honest, manly wine is a never-ending source of surprise.

AUSTRIAN DUCKHAMSTARTER

The celebrated blue wine of Austria which not only kicks like a mule but helps you start on those cold mornings.

KNOW YOUR WINOS

A GUIDE TO SAMPLERS

LE POSEUR

LE DEAN MARTIN

LE GOBBEUR

LE PISS-ARTISTE SERIEUX

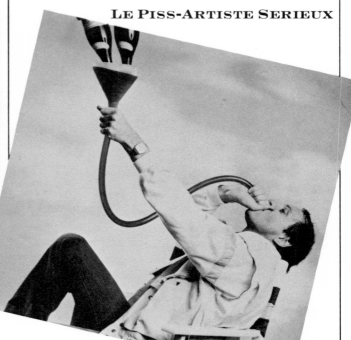

INSOMNIA

ere's a chapter purely for those people who suffer from insomnia. If you've never suffered from insomnia move on to the next chapter.

It's an interesting affliction, insomnia. It strikes me about every three or four months and it lasts for approximately three or four months. I'm not too sure what causes it, in fact I have no idea – I lie awake in bed for hours wondering about it.

Insomnia is a solo affliction, no matter how many people in bed at one time, insomnia will only strike one person. It never affects two people in bed at the same time. It's very infuriating being wide awake at 3 a.m. in the morning when you can't get to sleep knowing that your partner is rock-solid out. Not only are they rock-solid out, they are zedding away with enough noise to wake the whole street.

Of course you try and wake them. A good large dig in the sides with your elbow will elicit some sort of garbled response and restless wriggling, etc. Eventually with enough digging they'll actually say something intelligible like, 'Hold it, hold it, the bread's in the middle of the road.' A further nudge will elicit something like, 'Hang on, hang on, the bicycle's on top of the fridge and shining on my knees.' People talk absolute garbage when they are asleep. Also, nothing wakes them. That is, until *you* are asleep and then they hear a mouse in the garden move a pebble. 'What's that? What's that?' they cry. 'It's burglars, what is it? What's that noise?' You awaken from your deep slumber going, 'What noise? What noise? What burglar?' to turn round and find your partner rock-solid out, zedding away by the side of you.

I've tried many remedies to cure insomnia. I thought possibly it could be the bed itself. I went through king-size beds, single beds, double beds, double-sprung mattresses, double-edged – every conceivable kind of blanket and duvet, Japanese futons, etc. I even bought a water bed, and the first night I was rather careless and left the electric blanket on and woke up in the morning poached.

The problem for any insomniac is – what to do with the hands? These are very awkward appendages and never rest comfortably anywhere on or about the person. To stop myself going blind, I cut two large holes right through the bed so I could stick my arms through them and sleep with my head on the mattress while the arms fiddled about on the floor. This is okay until you *do* fall asleep and turn over in the middle of the night. You then have a ruddy great bed on top of you suffocating you to death.

Another problem with insomniacs is what to think about. You do have literally hours upon hours upon hours to think. The end of the world and the meaning of life is easy-peasy to an insomniac. True insomniacs actually go off on obscure tangents like, 'If you unscrew your navel, will your bum fall off?', 'Why do Kamikaze pilots wear helmets?' and so on. I heard a classic statement on Radio Four. Some professor who was in Mensa or something asked the question, 'If a tree falls over in a forest and there's no one there, does it make a sound?' After much consideration and many hours of sleeplessness, I thought, what a prat. Still, when you belong to Mensa you think about these sort of things. I myself can't wait to be in Mensa. It will mean I have an IQ over 148 and can answer all those fundamental problems of life like, 'What's the odd one out between a lion, Weybridge High Street, *Woman's Own* and a fly?' and the answer is – a fly, because it's the only one that will pass through a tennis racquet. You have to go to insomniacs for this sort of information, you don't find it in *Encyclopaedia Britannica*.

So, for all insomniacs reading this chapter, you probably wish that you had skipped it in the first place.

MURDOCH TO MERGE SUN WITH TIMES IN COST-CUTTING MOVE

The Sun Times says

CALL FOR RAMBO!

So the most irrelevant man in Britain, Neil 'Baldilocks' Kinnock has finally plucked up the courage to say what the nation is thinks. Backed up by the yobs, commies and loonies of his back benches, he dares to ask the greatest Prime Minister of all time if the economy will ever be in the black.

Marvellous Maggie has three well-chosen words for the Welsh windbag. 'Search me, squire,' she said.

Today your No. 1 *Times* says what the nation is thinking.

Why don't you urinate off, you pathetic little git. Otherwise we'll lock you away in a darkened room and invite Rambo over to beat the living faeces out of you.

Then the good ship Maggie could get back to ruling the country without irrelevant interruptions.

SALUTE THIS HERO

In the space of seven days, one man has managed the impossible. He has closed down three printers, merged the *Sun* with the soaraway *Times*, put in a takeover for that bankrupt national joke the BBC, and shifted a hell of a lot of money out of this country and into a safe account in Liechtenstein.

That's what we call a good week's work.

Isn't it about time that Britain rewarded its entrepreneurs instead of criticizing them? Why not GIVE this great man the BBC and save us all the ruinous expense of the licence fee NOW?

We'd make one further suggestion – in four brief words.

Arise, Sir Rupert Murdoch.

A GOOD THRASHING

So the Minister of Sport thinks that better policing and identity cards are the answer to football violence. What a wimp.

Every right-minded person loathes and despises the violence that has become the most important

not give these yobs a taste of the blood the lash until the courses in rivulets down their spotty legs into their Doc Martens?

That would soon teach them the most important

Britain's liveliest letters

LETTERS TO THE EDITOR

Over the top

Sir, My wife took one look at the sparkling new-style *Sun Times* and came up with the priceless comment: 'It's not the top people's paper these days – it's the topless people's!!!

Seriously though, folks, keep up the great work.

Yours sincerely,
ADMIRAL SIR JOHN
SKEFFINGTON-LODGE,
Skeffington Lodge, Wilts

Thanks, Admiral!

Victoria public house featured in the 'EastEnders' television series into a late-hour drinking club and disco.

Concerning the BBC's alleged intention to 'clean up' the sex and violence in the series, in particular the saucy antics of 'Dirty' Den, we would stress the need for the fullest public soundings, extending even to a Parliamentary Select Committee to study the implications of such a serious development before placing at risk such a vital part of our great national heritage.

Yours sincerely,

LORD CHALFONT OF
FLEET
RT HON DAVID OWEN MP
MISS SU POLLARD
LORD DENNING QC
MR DAVID
ATTENBOROUGH

Glorious heritage

Sir, In view of the continuing speculation in your 'Fabulous World of Showbiz' column, we the undersigned would like to place on record our profound reservations concerning the proposed conversion of the saloon lounge in the Queen

MR 'BOB' GELDOF
HIS GRACE THE DUKE OF
NORFOLK
MR DENNIS SKINNER MP
MR 'DIRTY' DEN
LADY YOUNG OF
KENSINGTON
MR STEPHEN 'CHINLESS'
WONDER
ORVILLE
THE MARQUIS OF
BLANDFORD
MR LESLIE CROWTHER

Splittin' mad

Sir, Is George Michael's new No. 1 hit single 'I Want To Really Make It With You' the first time a split infinitive has reached the top of the charts?

Quis custodiet . . .?

Yours sincerely,
MR KEITH RICHARD
'Dunscorin',
Henley-on-Thames

DEIRDRE'S DAILY DRAMA

'For years, I've believed that my marriage was no different, from any other in this country. I look after the family stockmarket portfolio, the children go to boarding school, the wife plans menus with Cook during the week, then beats me up dressed in Nazi uniform every Saturday night. But recently I've been feeling strange yearnings towards a young lad I happened to bump into at do at the Russian Embassy – yearnings which I haven't felt since I used to share a cold shower with 'Bummer' Blunt at Cambridge in the thirties. Igor – that's my young friend's name – tells me I'm

fussing unduly but I still feel so guilty. Also I hate the way he asks me to describe what we do in his Maida Vale flat in what he calls my sexy, BBC voice', and I can't understand why he has to go 'Testing one-two, testing one-two' at the end of the day. Is true love more important in life than national security or World War III?'

LT COL. 'SWISH-HIPS'
JOHNSTON,
Ministry of Defence, Whitehall

Deidre says:
Come off it, Swish-Hips – surely you're old enough to see that this Igor's up to no good.

You're simply going through the crisis that many other security chiefs in the Ministry of Defence have suffered from, entirely forgetting the consequences of their actions – the questions in the House, the scoop-hungry journalists asking smutty questions, the wife having to say 'I stand by my husband' every time she steps out of doors? Back to the Nazi uniform, Swishy, before we're obliged to blow the whistle on you. By the way, the editor remembers you at Eton and says you were a right little tart even then, so don't try to kid us that this is something new!!!

Wales of the week

Nina Myskow reviews the Royal Shakespeare Company production of *A Midsummer Night's Dream*.

If any of you culture-vultures have a mind to drop in on the RSC's latest effort, I've got some words of advice – stay at home, folks! 'Cos this ain't no Dream – it's a bleedin' Nightmare. If old Shakespeare had seen it, he'd have renamed himself 'the Bored of Avon'.

I have a message for the lumbering, overweight lads and lasses of the RSC: why the Puck don't you give up and move into a career more suited to your awesome talents – like extras for the Extremely Ugly Agency?

Hermia looked like she was suffering from one, Titania was carrying more surplus cellulite

than Big Daddy, and Bottom was just that – acres and acres of revolting bum-flesh that threatened to clear the stage of all other forms of life. Did I say life??? Forget it.

Sir Alec Guinnless, as Oberon, tries valiantly to bring some dignity to proceedings but frankly isn't he a bit old to be wrinkling about the stage in fancy dress, spouting old-fashioned blank verse?

And as for token hunk Jeremy Irons as Theseus – he looked quite dishy until he came on in tights – BIG mistake. Or rather, little mistake 'cos, to my seasoned eye, he looked distinctly light in the lunchbox area, as my old granny used to say! The acting, direction and sets were probably quite good, but I was too busy noting down jokes about the actors' physical defects to bother about them.

In short, this production got right on my Titanias. Oberon out!

Nina Myskow

COURT AND SOCIAL

Mr Terry Wogan will not be sending any Christmas cards this year.

Lovely Miss June Papworth is pleased to announce that, as from Monday night, she is involved in a steamy love tangle with a famous Radio One disc jockey.

Mr Chris Quinten, the Street's own Mr Love-Machine, will attend the opening of Princess Dai, Mr Dai

Llewellyn's new nightclub on Wednesday evening.

Following the saucy sex secrets revelations of the stars in yesterday's *Sun Times*, Mrs Betty Smith is pleased to make a shock wedding announcement on behalf of her daughter Suzy and a well-known Liverpool soccer star. The wedding will take place as soon as he's been found.

What a thighful! The television announcer Miss Selina Scott arrives at yesterday's royal garden party and gives us the chance to show you yet another picture of her legs. See page 9 for more Sunsational pics of HRH Princess Diana of Wales in THAT plunging neckline.

Twenty things you didn't know about Bernard Levin

1. Bernard Levin was born Gary Levin in Macclesfield. He started calling himself 'Bernard' quite late in life.

2. Contrary to popular belief, English is in fact his mother tongue.

3. Gary is not thought to have experienced childhood as we know it.

4. He did his national service in the Catering Corps, where he acquired the nickname 'Prunes'.

5. 'Prunes's' ambition on leaving the army was to be a stand-up comic, and he once auditioned unsuccessfully for Brian Rix's legendary 'Great British Laughter Show'.

6. He wrote a comic novel about life in the Catering Corps when he was in his twenties which he still hopes to get published 'one of these days'.

7. It was only when Bernard Braden declined to take part in 'That Was the Week That Was'

that 'Prunes' got his big break into showbiz.

8. He got so few laughs in his first appearance that producer Ned Sherrin decided to make him the show's 'resident intellectual'. It was at this point that he changed his name from 'Prunes' to 'Bernard', a name he chose out of respect for Braden.

9. 'Bernard' once attacked a live audience on TW3, beating them about the head and demanding to known why they had given him such a lousy round of applause.

10. He does not, in fact, like opera very much, preferring to unwind to the sounds of Leo Sayer, Barbra Streisand and The Blow Monkeys.

11. A lifelong bachelor, 'Bernard's' most intense relationship was with Nana Mouskouri, the ex-singing nun who is now the Greek Minister of Culture.

12. His favourite TV pro-

gramme is 'Star Trek'.

13. Somebody once mistook him for Henry Kissinger and poured a pot of white paint over him.

14. 'Bernard' drives a silver Aston Martin with a customized library.

15. When asked who his favourite comedian is, he likes to answer 'Neil Kinnock'. This is his only known joke.

16. He once joined the Hare Krishna movement, which believes in reincarnation. A Fleet Street wit commented, 'He must have done something pretty awful in an earlier life to be reincarnated as "Bernard' Levin!"

17. There aren't really twenty things that you didn't know about 'Bernard' Levin.

18. Although he would probably disagree with what I've just said.

19. Er, the Saudi Arabians have no word in their language for 'igloo'.

20. His

THE TEN MOST BORING QUESTIONS ASKED BY JOURNALISTS

1. What's your real name.

2. Who are your favourite comedians?

3. How did you start in the business?

4. How did you get that scar?

5. What's the most hilarious thing that's ever happened to you?

6. Do you prefer working live or on television?

7. Do you write all your own material?

8. When are you going to make a comeback?

9. Are you going to pay for this meal?

10. Do you mind sitting on this pile of carrots, biting the head off a mole as we rearrange the furniture in your lounge for a quick photograph?

TELEVISION'S LAST GREAT MYSTERY

I n these television-obsessed days, there's really nothing that we don't know about what goes on behind the scenes. There are *no* secrets – we know everything: Wogan's favourite deodorant, where Jimmy Savile buys his naff jewellery, the name of Jan Leeming's wig-maker . . .

Yet one mystery remains.

Where on earth do the BBC find their weathermen?

After all, you don't meet people like that in everyday life. Or at least, if you do, you wouldn't notice them and you certainly wouldn't say to yourself, 'Look at that cheap suit, that grey skin, that mousey little face – he'd look just great on television doing the weather!'

So where do they find them? For a time, it was thought that they used specially trained interviewers who roamed around the country, mixing incognito with the most boring commuters they could find. They'd travel in every day on, say, the 8.27 from Purley to Waterloo in the hope of finding a sufficiently boring and awkward-looking chap, with just the right kind of grating, whiny voice, to make the perfect BBC weather-forecaster.

The most popular BBC weatherman of all time was said to have been discovered this way, hiding behind his *Daily Telegraph* on his way to work as a small claims clerk for an insurance company. The BBC scout took one look at him – the crumpled Terylene suit, the National Health specs, the egg-stain on the faded blue tie, the apologetic, hunched shoulders – and realized that here was a natural, a star in the making.

'Excuse me,' said the man from the BBC. 'Could you just say after me "Scattered showers", please.'

'Scuttered shayowies,' he said.

'You're hired,' said the BBC man.

But apparently the new regime at the Corporation have decided that this method is simply too haphazard and time-consuming to be in keeping with its new, streamlined image – in future, the quest for the most boring men in Britain would be scientifically conducted with the help of the latest research equipment and high technology.

So now the polytechnics of Britain are scoured once a year for the people with so little charisma and charm that their mere appearance on television has a mesmeric effect on the average viewer.

It's not easy to get in – some extremely dull people have been turned down. It might have been a chance interesting remark or simply that they were wearing a rather nice tie. Any sign of originality is ruthlessly exposed by the BBC's sophisticated interviewing techniques.

But to help would-be weather-forecasters, some unofficial guidelines have been drawn up for candidates.

SO YOU WANT TO BE A WEATHER FORECASTER...

Here's how you can do it!

Take a look at the little chap who follows the BBC news any evening of the week. He's embarrassing, isn't he?

Yet that little divot is probably earning twice as much as you are. Not only that. He gets to appear in the *Mail on Sunday*. He chats with Julia Somerville in the BBC canteen. He cops £1000 for opening a supermarket. Grandmothers send him pairs of their knitted mittens.

Are you the sort of person who, faced with this kind of information simply says, 'Oh yes, each to his own,' and goes back to doing the *Daily Telegraph* quick crossword?

If so, we want to hear from you. Because quite possibly you're boring enough to become a BBC weatherman yourself.

But, before you dust the dandruff off your Harry Fenton suit and make your dreary way via the 9.21 from Hatch End, changing on the Central Line at Liverpool Street, alighting at the White City and make the final few yards by what the wife calls 'Shanks's pony' (she's the joker of the family!), take time to read these simple guidelines.

Because we're quite busy enough thinking up new ways of spending your licence money without wasting our time on interviewees who are even slightly interesting.

General appearance

The key word is 'grey'. Imagine the greyest city clerk returning home after a particularly grey day in a grey, smoke-filled office. Your skin should reflect the unpleasantly insipid colour of your suit. While you should look unhealthy, you should never look *so* unhealthy that you become interesting. You're the sort of person who suffers from piles and halitosis but who outlives everyone. If you happen to have cut yourself shaving (probably the most exciting moment of your day), stick a small piece of paper on the wound. A hint of acne is an advantage but nothing too spectacular, mind – a throbbing, glowing zit on the point of explosion may help draw attention to you.

Speech

Don't mumble. Being unintelligible might just give you an entirely undeserved air of mystery. Viewers need to be able to hear *exactly* how dull you are.

On the other hand, do *not* come on like Ruislip's answer to Larry Olivier or, if you happen to think you're a bit of a card, John Cleese. A dull grating noise should emanate from you – as undramatic as you like, but naggingly annoying. Think of a solicitor reading out a will that contains nothing but bad news for everyone and you'll be on the right track.

Regional accents are not acceptable since many people find mad Celts a bit more interesting than a little nerd from the Home Counties.

Vocabulary

Wherever possible use clichés that are as dull and overused as your tie. So you mustn't grumble, takes all sorts, worse things happen at sea, what's yours, the lady wife, take a pew, this is it, I'll have a pint of what you're having, cheers, etc., etc.

Character

You should not have one of these.

Posture

Until recently, a slightly cringing droop of the shoulders was all that was required. But, following the success of Ian MacCaskill, the more active 'bob and weave' approach has become popular. Simply behave as if the cameraman was about to start throwing snowballs at you or someone's smeared Deep Heat inside your loins.

Family life

Your wife should be 'something of a home bird'. You should have two children who are so faceless that even the double glazing salesman can't be bothered to remember their names. Their idea of a family treat should be a round trip of motorway bridges.

Outside interests

If you have to have outside interests, make sure that there's nothing that even the most desperate journalist will consider worth reporting. Model trains are good, so is 'cooking Sunday lunch for the family'. The occasional game of park football is acceptable, so long as you show no talent whatsoever and play in a thoroughly boring position, floating around ineffectually on the wing.

Note for women applicants

While we could in no way be described as being sexist, we feel it is only fair to point out that there is as much chance of women applicants being accepted as there is of Lord Lucan riding Shergar in the Derby.

We learnt our lesson from Barbara Edwards, who looked ordinary enough but turned out to have hidden depths and secret interests. We can elaborate no further.

Other BBC leaflets in this series

Your hair-style could get *you* a job as a newscaster!

Could *you* be stupid enough to be a game-show host?

Do *you* like big lunches, sucking up to politicians, taking long holidays and seeing your name in the papers? Tough – we got there first.

GEMINI

Some say there's an
unfortunate hitch in
The Gemini person's head.
They come to the boil in the
kitchen
But barely simmer in bed.

CANCER

The only interesting Cancer
That I've met in my life to this
day
Was a bald-headed bottomless
dancer
Plying his trade in Bridlington
Bay.

AN ADDRESS TO TREKKIES, ASSEMBLED IN BIRMINGHAM FOR THE TWENTIETH ANNIVERSARY MEETING OF THE STAR TREK CONVENTION

It's not often I get the chance to meet other extraterrestrials en bloc like this. As you know, the earthlings have a great capacity to restrict the benefits of our alien origins and it's a great relief to spend the next few days amongst similar oppressed kind.

As this is my first convention please forgive me if I'm a little rusty on the inter-galactic greeting signs, extraterrestrials being in short supply in Birmingham. One gets out of the habit so easily. I had the usual embarrassing experience last month when exchanging greetings with someone I thought was from the planet Zog. We were going through the arcane Zoggite recognition ritual — you know, the intertwined wrists and treble finger stroke hop on one foot and side head-butt routine — when it started to dawn on me that he was a freemason. Now which one of us hasn't been through this experience before?

It's when they start demanding your lodge number and what size apron you wear that things get difficult. At times like these you wish you were from Krypton and could resort to the old Vesuvian trick of feigning stupidity. 'Gluck gluck,' I shouted, splaying my legs out from the knees and clutching my chin from behind. Curiously this seemed to confirm his suspicions of my non-initiation to the brotherhood. He called for immediate

assistance from his fellow masons, and as the policemen approached I had to do a very smart piece of manoeuvring to escape.

I think it is very important at this convention to discuss ways of freeing ourselves from the drugs the earthlings cunningly force us to eat to stop us being brilliant, particularly the dreaded mono-sodium glutamate and even worse the addictive Mars Bar. How ironic that the docile organic people of Mars should have their planet associated with this alien suppressant. (Note there is a recuperation unit situated in the hotel foyer for anyone OD-ing on Chinese food, Mars Bars or other similar confectionary.)

This deliberate suppression of our natural cosmic ability to de-materialize, move about invisibly, play Trivial Pursuit and generally rule the planet Earth has got to stop. Do not be fooled by people telling you, that you are just ego-obsessed, living in a fantasy world, that we are just HUMAN (hah) like everyone else. We are aliens and should be proud of it.

The lengths these humans will go to to assure us that we are just one of them and that we live on a normal round planet! Australia, they say, is on the other side of the world. Phoowee! This is a flat slab of asteroid and they know it. I thought, I'll call their bluff, and purchased a ticket to go to Australia. That sent them panicking! They had to keep me locked up in a plane for twenty-four hours, on the pretence of flying there to give them time to transform Brighton into Bondi Beach and Luton into Adelaide.

I must admit they accomplished it very well indeed — clever fellows these Homo sapiens, don't underestimate them.

Still I'm sure we can match them for deviousness. The very fact you yourselves have been secretly meeting for twenty years under the guise of Star Trek conventions shows how gullible the earth Mind Police are.

The fact that I, 'Gabloid', from the planet Swish, have only just heard about it is indicative of how successful you have been.

The extraterrestrials in Birmingham have had to be equally inventive. They're helped by the fact they tend to be clanish. Do you remember the long-suffering inhabitants of Kramavon? How they had to watch their planet slowly dying from lack of atmosphere? How the inherent skills of the populace vanished and died forever as each year the crops failed? How in desperation they actually started to celebrate such events? Well, you will find the Kramavons at Birmingham City's football ground. There's not many left now since the deity 'Trevor the Francis' was energized to Sampdoria. They should be approached with caution and not a little sympathy. A friendly greeting like 'Can I buy your season ticket?' will go a long way towards encouraging intergalactic fraternal greetings.

The Klingons are represented here in their usual comic guise of double-glazing salesmen, as are the Estarte Agentus, the slimy inhabitants of Pluto.

One word of warning. There is a particularly powerful black hole situated in the centre of Birmingham. It is known locally as the Bull Ring. Once motorized vehicles enter this phenomenon, they are rarely if ever seen again. On the infrequent occasions when their inhabitants do emerge they are said to be spinning out of control with glazed eyes or savagely attacking an AA patrolman.

What happens in the very centre of the hole is as yet unknown. What happens to the material that gets sucked in is a matter of conjecture. Some say it is de-molecularized, passed through energy channels to reappear at the other black hole nearby, 'Spaghetti Junction'. Others claim it is energy and raw material for the HP Sauce factory in Aston. Who knows? Spock would sort it out if he was here — until then, be warned!

So on behalf of all Birmingham aliens, I wish you a successful and secret convention. I'm sure I will be able to join you, it's just that I'm having a little trouble at present duplicating the key the earth man uses to lock the door.

Besides which it's very difficult working your arms in these silly jackets.

GABLOID
Ward 111
Earth name Jasper Carrott

58

CENSORED SCENES FROM MY AUTOBIOGRAPHY
I WAS SCARGY'S DOUBLE

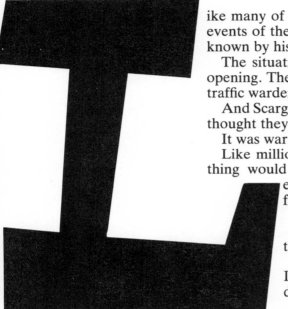

ike many of my fellow countrymen, I was confused and angered by the events of the long, miserable winter of '83 – the time which came to be known by historians as 'the long, miserable winter of '83'.

The situation was intolerable. Pits were closing. Soup kitchens were opening. The police were so overstretched that a platoon of metropolitan traffic wardens were said to be holding Ravenscraig single-handedly.

And Scargill and Macgregor were on the 'News at Ten' so often viewers thought they were newscasters.

It was war. It was hell. Worse than that, it was very, very boring.

Like millions of people all over the country, I wished that the whole thing would go away and that the British way of life could be re-established, with snooker on the telly, the Royal Family on the front pages, and just the occasional riot to liven things up a bit.

But what could I do?

Little did I know that I was about to play a key role in one of the most astonishing episodes in our glorious island's history.

It all started one cold night in January. The phone rang. My daughter answered it.

'It's Arthur Scargill for you,' she said.

I picked up the receiver, my heart beating like a truncheon on a riot shield.

'Carrott?' said the voice at the other end. 'Scargy here!'

'Get away,' I said nervously. 'You're not, are you?'

'Listen.' He cleared his throat. 'Because *frankly* we are *not* prepared to negotiate over the wholesale *butchery* of the coal-mining industry as we know it.'

It was unmistakable, that grating, high-pitched Yorkshire whine. Incredible as it seemed, I was talking to Scargy himself.

'How can I help you, Scargy?' I asked nervously.

'Get on't bike down to t' headquarters and 'appen I'll tell you,' he said, and hung up . . . (Sorry, I'm not that good at Yorkshire accents).

The Planning Room at the National Union of Mineworkers – 'the Court of King Arthur' as the *Daily Mail* called it – was every bit as impressive as I'd expected.

It was a huge hall, festooned with union emblems and banners. There was a bar at one end, with genuine sawdust on the Wilton carpet.

There was a good, honest, manly smell about the place – a heady mixture of beer and shag. I've always thought that there's nothing quite like a heady mixture of beer and shag to make a man feel at home.

By a huge, roaring coal fire (one of the few in the country at that time) sat Scargy, with a retinue of men in ill-fitting suits and toupees.

'Ah, Carrott,' he said. 'Sit thee down lad and make theesel' right comfortable.' He motioned to a small footstool near his feet.

'Jasper,' he said. 'What would you say if I told you that several people have remarked on the extraordinary facial similarity between us?'

'I'd say they'll be hearing from my lawyers in the morning.'

A sudden hush fell on the room. Scargy smiled thinly. 'Very funny, Jasper,' he said. 'I like a joke. We all like a joke, don't we, lads?' His followers tittered nervously. 'Yes, people say that the resemblance between us is – ' Scargy paused dramatically for effect ' – striking.'

The room exploded with laughter which continued until Scargy held up his hand. It was then that he unveiled his devilish plan. It was daring, dangerous – foolhardy even.

Yet it could just work . . .

Many of you will remember that the grimmest aspect of those dark days – grimmer even than a full-length televized press conference held by Ian Macgregor – was something called The Miners Benefit.

At The Miners Benefit, a lot of Londoners in smart denims threw £5 notes into buckets for the privilege of feeling that they were part of the class struggle. Their punishment was to have to sit through three hours of alternative entertainment provided by celebrities who felt their radical profile needed a lift.

The acts were always the same.

There'd be a bunch of people singing without a backing group.

There'd be a male alternative comedian with a radical three-day beard making jokes about lager and Norman Tebbit.

There'd be a teenybopper band miming to their latest hit.

There'd be a female alternative comedian doing non-sexist routines about period pains and men's genitals.

Then, and most important of all, there'd be Scargy. Or at least, they thought it was Scargy. In fact, Scargy was well away from it all, discussing how best to shift the NUM's money around the banks of Europe so fast that no court could catch it.

It was me who took the bows. Me who waved to row upon row of wine-bar wallies with phony accents. Me who made the statutory speech about the wholesale butchery of the coal-mining industry as we know it.

For I was Scargy's double . . .

It got predictable. Well things do, don't they?

I had my own life to lead. A new television series, a trip to America, a book maybe.

It was time to move on . . .

I'll never forget the faces on the men in grey at the National Coal Board when I strode in unannounced to deliver my bombshell.

For one moment I thought Ian Macgregor was going to wake up from his

slumbers at the head of the long table, but he merely stirred, muttered an American obscenity which I'd never heard before, and went back to sleep.

'Good God,' said one of his henchmen. 'I don't believe it. It's – '

'Yes,' I said, bristling my newly grown Scargy sideboards.

'It's Robert Mitchum isn't it?'

''Appen it's not, by thee breeches,' I said, taking a deep breath. 'We are *not* prepared to negotiate over – '

'Scargy!' It was Macgregor who had woken with a start. 'Help, arrest him! The enemy within! Call the cops! It's the anti-Christ!'

'At your service,' I smiled.

'What d'you want, Scargy?' hissed one of the men in grey.

'I want to negotiate,' I said.

'But what about the wholesale butchery of the coal-mining industry as we know it?'

'I've . . . I've had second thoughts. 'Appen a bit of butchery wouldn't be quite so bad after all. . . .'

The rest is history.

Before the real Scargy could explain what had happened, the crisis was over.

Pits re-opened. Soup kitchens closed. Traffic wardens laid down their riot shields. The country returned to snooker, the Royal Family and some rather good riots.

Scargy made it up with me over a jar at the Olde Pithead Ballot.

He even offered to do a nationwide tour in my place, giving me a reasonable cut of the take if I'd sit in on the occasional NUM meeting.

But that's another story. . . .

HAPPY HOUR

A quick review of currently fashionable cocktails

THE SLOW COMFORTABLE SCREW

A cocktail that is extremely popular with men from the Pru and other society do-gooders.

Ingredients: Drambuie to numb the brain. Rum and advocaat to numb the feet so that you can't walk away. A dissolved anabolic steroid to activate your signing arm. And finally stout.

Aim: To convince you of the sheer common sense of the life-insurance service. Pay the insurance company lots of money and they give it all back to you. When you die.

THE HUMP BUMP AND GRIND

Aim: To be certain your partner comes across.

Instructions: Strap victim to back of lounge chair, tilt head back and insert car jack between teeth. Extend car jack fully. Into said orifice, pour anything over 11% proof until liquid overflows out of nose. Insert large pineapple to block up mouth and two cherries up nostrils. Transfer victim to laundromat spin dryer. Eject after a good twenty minutes and force Dyno Rod vibrating pole down the victim's throat to ensure drink refreshes parts that other cocktails cannot reach.

THE WHAT THE....

Ingredients: Horlicks, Milk of Magnesia, Angostura bitters, Domestos decorated with anchovies and spinach.

Result: Always has the effect on your partner of saying 'What the…', thereby encouraging a more normal, less expensive drink the next time round.

LA DOUCHE CHIEN FATALE

Aim: A devious French invention aimed at exporting more nonsense to us.

Ingredients: Highly carbonated ten-year-old Beaujolais Nouveau mixed with onion liqueur, very runny Brie and that special brandy that blows the wax out of a St Bernard's ears.

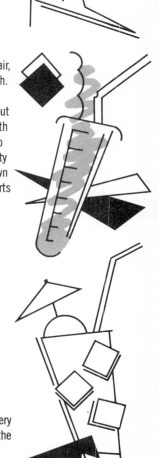

TRADITIONAL CRAFTS OF THE EIGHTIES

No. 11 The Meter Maid

Occasionally, during the latter part of the twentieth century, an overenthusiastic politician would manage to convince the British people that the rest of the world was right and that everybody should stop enjoying themselves and start working for a living. As a result, extremely ugly office blocks were erected in the centre of cities and so-called 'commuters' had nervous breakdowns trying to drive into work every day, littering the once tranquil streets of Britain's conurbations with executive saloons, continental hatchbacks and town runabouts for the little lady. Roads were choked, pavements blocked, the normal business of the city – going to the betting shop, mugging the tourists, getting ratarsed down The Lame Duck – came to a shuddering halt. What could be done?

The answer was the arrival of the meter maid. Like other traditional crafts of the eighties, the meter maids would hang around the city streets wearing distinctive clothes and touting for custom – but their custom was illegally parked cars.

Sombre as their task was, many of the meter maids engaged in playful practices to enliven their day. They would 'book' cars parked for three minutes in particularly harmless places, ignoring those blocking a main road. They would reduce drivers to quivering, impotent wrecks by giving them a ticket just as they were returning to their cars to drive away. It was said by meter maids that, once they had started to write out a ticket, nothing short of an Act of God – and sometimes not even that – could prevent them from completing it.

With the introduction of clamping, meter maids were rapidly phased out, often taking up work as prison warders, abbattoir operatives or Electrical Appliance Officers for the Bolivian Secret Police. Nowadays, the few raddled old hags kitted out in yellow and black, who appear at the annual Lord Mayor's Show in London are all that is left to remind us of the glorious heyday of the meter maid.

No. 4 The Telephone Vandal

With his short-cropped hair, neanderthal forehead and familiar street cry, ''Ere we go, 'Ere we go, 'Ere we go', the telephone vandal was a familiar sight around the cities of Merrie England during the 1980s.

EXHIBIT A

'Vandalizing' – the practice of rendering a public telephone box entirely useless by acts of violence and extreme unpleasantness – grew into prominence as an art form during the 1970s. By the following decade, it had become such a popular pastime that any public telephone from which calls could still be made was regarded as such a rare and precious object that people would travel from miles around and then queue for hours simply to experience at least once in their lives a public telephone that actually made calls.

Naturally, telephone vandals would often join the queue, cunningly disguised as normal people. Once inside they would make a couple of obscene calls, relieve themselves and then set about destroying the kiosk with a few swift head butts. The rest of the queue would then drift away disconsolately in a vain search for another public telephone box, or even a bus shelter with some glass in it.

What induced vandals to deface and destroy public telephones? Was it an eloquent, human protest against the creeping mechanization of Western society? A comment on a telephone system that would have disgraced the island of Tonga? A 'self-expression through direct action' exhibition sponsored by the Arts Council? Or sheer pig ignorance?

Whatever the truth, telephone vandalism died out in the early 1990s when, following the privatization of British Telecom, the kiosks were sold off to local councils to help ease the housing shortage. Ironically, many vandals found that their entire families had been relocated by the council to a kiosk that they themselves had once vandalised.

Soon yet another traditional craft of the eighties had been consigned to the history books.

No. 23 The VATman*

It is not easy for us today to believe that, not so very long ago, there still walked the streets of Great Britain little grey-suited men with cheap mackintoshes, Woolworth briefcases and angry eyes, who

EXHIBIT C

could tell you what 3/23 of any sum was without even thinking.

They were called VATmen.

VATmen became a feature of British life in the grim, dark days of the 1970s, shortly after a minor civil servant in the Treasury earned himself a knighthood and an index-linked pension for life by inventing an entirely new way for the government to fleece the public. At first, he called it the TBE – Tax on Bloody Everything – but after several cabinet meetings and a special Tax on Bloody Everything Select Committee it was decided that this was a bit obvious and that the name of VAT – Value Added Tax – was less likely to be rumbled by the voters.

The VATmen were recruited from the lower echelons of the civil service, the only three requirements for instant employment being:

1. A deep and abiding affection for remittance notes, bank statements, receipts and similar wastepaper products.
2. A deep and abiding grudge against the whole human race, in particular those smart enough to earn a bit of cash for themselves.
3. The ability to multiply by 3/23s.

Like witches in the Middle Ages or press gangs during the sixteenth century, VATmen were feared visitors in the Britain of the late 1980s. Many was the household startled by the unscheduled arrival on the doorstep of a little man with angry eyes, a plastic briefcase and dandruff.

'I am the man from the VAT and I have a warrant to ruin your day,' the man would say.

'*Shizerhund!* – it's the soddin' VATman,' the householder would traditionally respond as the grey-suited zombie brushed past him, demanding full documentation covering inputs, outputs, offputs, offcuts and a cup of tea with two sugars would be very welcome, thank you very much.

So to those who talk of 'the good old days', one reply is sufficient. 'You mean the good old days of VAT!!!' It was, after all, the VATman who, during those dismal days, coined the phrase that became among the most feared in the English language.

'Have you got a receipt for that, sir?'

---

* Some historians believe that 'VATwomen' existed but, given the charmlessness and low moral character of 'VATpeople' generally, this appears unlikely.

No. 16 The Stripogram Artiste

Imagine for a moment that you are a young lad trembling on the brink of matrimony in the year of 1986. Your friends at the office have taken you out to a cheap and noisy restaurant for the most popular pre-marriage rite of the time, the stag party.

At the height of proceedings, you are mildly surprised to be accosted at your table by a big, loud-mouthed blonde, dressed up as a schoolgirl. Silence descends on the restaurant as she reads from her prepared script.

For little Jimmy I'm here to see
For this Saturday he will married be
But before our friend is now betrothed
For him I would like to be unclothed
I bring him luck, I think it's right
To give him something to remember for his first
night
So Jim, before you enter married bliss
Let me give you my special kiss
Then open your eyes and open your arms
And get a load of all my lovely charms.

To raucous cheers from the rest of your party, the blonde then peels off her skimpy garments and dances around a bit without any clothes, before sitting heavily on your lap. Horribly embarrassed but trying not to seem a bad sport, you allow her to play with your tie, tweak your nipples and nibble your earlobes.

The humiliation only ends when she sweeps up her clothes and disappears off to the ladies to prepare for another assignment.

The stripogram business was first launched in 1983 as a novel way of delivering messages. The service provided by British Telecom was notoriously unreliable and by using stripograms at least the telegram would be delivered. Getting shouted at by a naked woman was usually regarded as the price to be paid for an efficient service.

It soon became clear that the concept of public displays of the female body, without the slightest danger of actual contact of a human or sexual kind, was entirely in keeping with the tastes of the 1980s Englishman. Stripograms became a boom industry and the variety of freakish human offerings became enormous, encompassing Stripping Vicars, Fat

Lady-o-grams, Schoolgirl-o-grams, Thatchergrams, Rambograms (which involved being hit hard by a violent, semi-naked muscleman), Naughty Nunograms, Wrinklograms (also known as Granograms), Princess Dianagrams, Dwarfograms and so on.

There were several attempts to ban this bizarre trade in human humiliation, a sort of twentieth-century version of the old circus freak show, but, in keeping with its belief in free enterprise and the rights of the small businessman to make a fast buck, the government did nothing.

It was finally the blaze of publicity surrounding the

so-called Stripogram funeral that did for this unhappy trade. The funeral of a senior and well-loved Conservative councillor in the borough of Kensington, London was marred by a clerical error which led to the ceremony being taken by a young actor called Timothy Beaver, who was earning extra money as a Stripping Vicar.

As the coffin entered the packed church, the vicar announced in a loud voice, 'This poor old fart's just passed away/But don't worry ladies, I'll make your day' and proceeded to strip off his vestments. It was some time before the naked vicar was felled by a flying tackle from a local Young Conservative to be taken, still proudly unfrocked, to a nearby constabulary.

What was it all about? Were our forbears so frustrated, so warped, so ill at ease with their own sexual natures, that they derived some kind of release from watching unfortunates display themselves humiliatingly in public? Alas, it appears to be the case and must be regarded as yet another reason why the 1980s were very far from being the golden decade to which contemporary commentators liked to refer.

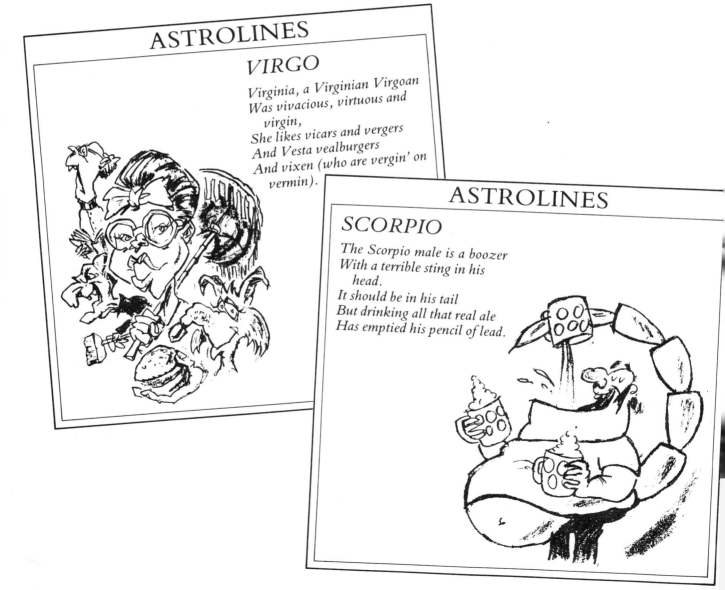

ASTROLINES

VIRGO

*Virginia, a Virginian Virgoan
Was vivacious, virtuous and
    virgin,
She likes vicars and vergers
And Vesta vealburgers
And vixen (who are vergin' on
    vermin).*

ASTROLINES

SCORPIO

*The Scorpio male is a boozer
With a terrible sting in his
    head.
It should be in his tail
But drinking all that real ale
Has emptied his pencil of lead.*

SOME COMPLETELY GRATUITOUS SEX AND VIOLENCE

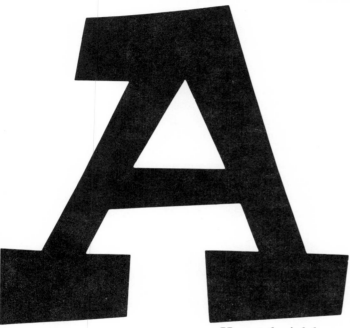s you know, there's a campaign going on to get rid of violence on television. . . . The campaign is pretty violent.

In my experience, most of the violence goes on behind the cameras. Television bosses kick hell out of producers, producers kick hell out of writers, and the unions kick hell out of everybody. Mary Whitehouse is watching the wrong end of the tube.

In any case, the thinking behind the protest is all wrong. The theory is that kids watch Karl Malden shoot down somebody in the streets of San Francisco, and immediately say, 'Let's go and shoot somebody down in Eastbourne.'

It doesn't work out that way. In the first place Karl Malden can't shoot anybody down because of all those noses he's got on his face. Every time he squints down the sights of his gun, at least two noses are in the way. If he pushes them to one side with his hand, his hand is in the way.

He got the job because he was the only actor willing to wear a blue mack in San Francisco, where the average daytime temperature is eighty-five degrees.

In the second place, intelligent kids would never shoot residents of Eastbourne . . . they know only too well that if they wait a few days the residents of Eastbourne will drop down dead on their own.

Where does this violence come in? Ah! American cop series!

But wait a minute! How can American cop series be *real* if they manage to solve every crime in sixty minutes minus four commercials? Well, they have a trick. The hero can't solve it, because he's too busy driving around in his Camaro and chatting up cleavage suspects round a pool. Sooner or later they have to bring in the person with the *information*. It's usually an ugly weedy guy, or an ugly female secretary.

Our macho hero is annoyed at being interrupted. He has his arm draped round this turn-out from the Revlon factory and says something petulantly like, 'What is it now, Peabody?'

And Peabody says, 'Sorry, Chief. But our computer read-out says that Muggsy Malone made a deal with Lomax when they shared a cell in Leavenworth to make Goldie the beneficiary, and when she hooked up with Gellini he put out a contract on Muggsy figuring a doublecross. . . .'

Our macho hero says, 'So Senator Fullbright was behind this after all!'

And we buy it! It's all Never-Never Land. So why should we believe the violence? Where else but on 'The A-Team' will you see fifty men firing automatic weapons at each other at point-blank range, and the only casualty is George Peppard's quiff?

Maybe I've got it wrong. I should have said that the campaign is not against violence, but *sex* and violence. The campaigners insist that the two be coupled together – like fish and chips, Laurel and Hardy, award ceremonies and nausea we have sex and violence.

Before the campaign, nobody thought of being violent when they had sex. . . . Now everybody does. Well, they go together don't they? Ageing couples, as they cut the golden wedding cake and give each other a kiss, grapple for the knife to see who can disembowel who for the sake of the cameras. Mild-mannered curates, for the same reason, bang choirboys over the bonce with the chalice before holding their hands.

The public now realize, thanks to the educative powers of television, that you can't have sex without violence; and it will only be a matter of time before they realize you can't have violence without sex . . .

When that day arrives, opposing armies will throw down their arms and indulge in a mass orgy, thus saving the world. That would be fine except we would have to put up with all the glut of ensuing war memoirs with titles like *Deep Threat* or *Cruising with Sam*.

Still, I can't help thinking the campaigners haven't made out a case. Okay, there's a bit of violence on television when they show news shots of the January sales. But sex?

Sex on television is simulated – it doesn't actually take place. All that writhing and panting malarky is just very good acting. I dare say the odd actor/actress takes advantage of the situation and starts wrapping the tongue round the tonsils, but in the main they fake it. That's why you end up with those ridiculous post-coital bedroom scenes in Clint Eastwood and James Bond movies. There is *he* – all bare and hairy-chested smoking a cigarette. And there's *she*, STWOHB (Sheets Tightly Wrapped Over Her Bosom). Then she clambers out of bed, still STWOHB, taking all the bedclothes with her. Why should she suddenly turn all demure in the morning, when they've both been humping all night long in the altogether?

No. The real danger of subliminal erotica is in the wildlife programmes. There's no faking it there. Spiders, ants, wildebeest, elephants – it's there for everyone to see any hour of the day or night, all channels, full colour. Not for them the agonizing scream and fingernails being drawn down the back – no, they look as if they actually *enjoy* it! *That's* the danger.

Why talk about television at all? It isn't television the way Logie Baird invented it. He spent his whole life tinkering about with lamps, flickers and

beams, to bring us live pictures *here* at the same time as it was happening over *there*.

'Och!' he exclaimed, as he inserted another fanwheel into a sprocket. 'Ye may scoff noo. But when I've finished, ye'll be able to see Liverpool play Everton and Leeds play Newcastle as the game is going on, in your own homes.' (I really am bad at accents.)

And he did too! But that's not the way it's turned out. All we see now is a succession of commentators in duffle coats, standing in empty stadiums after everybody has gone home saying, 'You should have been here! It was a fantastic match!'

Poor old Logie must be turning in his grave. There is so very little *live* television any more (the whole point of inventing it) – it's all taped. Most of it years ago. Even the news. There is so much news on tape, it will take years before we catch up with what's happening today. We're all living in the past. Jan Leeming is seventy-five years old. Ken Livingstone is Prime Minister, and J.R. is President of the United States, but that's not due to be shown until 1998.

They could have scrubbed round television altogether and just sold us videotape machines. Nobody wants to know what's going on *now*, it's all too nasty. Let's see it in ten years time, it'll be better then!

That's why the videotape machine companies have moved into the snob market.

The latest Model 2470 Havabashi V.T.R.! Records twelve hours of programming up to a month ahead!

It sounds fantastic. It certainly scores higher on the one-upmanship scale than the personalized registration plate. I never rated the latter. Why pay £2000 for a number plate with your initials, when for £100 you can buy any old plate, and change your name to fit the initials by deed-poll?

But hang on a minute. 'Records twelve hours of programming up to a month ahead'? Where are we going to find twelve hours in a month *worth* recording? Haven't the Japanese *seen* our television? We'd be hard put to find twelve hours in a year. And besides, where are we going to find out what's on television in a month's time? We can't find it in the newspapers or the magazines. Try phoning the television companies perhaps? Oh come on – that would be like phoning directory enquiries for a telephone number.

The whole macho-video image starts to crumble. It takes an engineering degree to record one hour ahead, let alone twelve. The machine looks like the control panel of Concorde. When I record a movie I can never find it. I get bits of 'Wogan', the news, 'Panorama', 'Wogan', and poetry readings from Glyndebourne – introduced by Wogan. But no movie. Somewhere I've pressed the wrong button.

I can't make head nor tail of it. I don't know what the older folks make of it. The other night my father-in-law watched a slow-motion replay of Robson missing a goal and said, 'If they let that lad play at his own pace he'd score.'

So that leaves us with TV commercials. I can give you a bit of background material here. Some time ago I was called in as a consultant on a committee which had a general as a chairman. They asked me a lot of security questions first like, 'Are both your parents British?' 'Have you spent any time within the Eastern bloc?' 'Were you ever Chinese?' And so on.

It turned out that they wanted to test my reaction as an ordinary viewer.

According to them, for some years now, Earth had been taken over by a Superior Intelligence.

I said, 'Good God! Where are they? If they're a Superior Intelligence they couldn't have taken over the government. We would have noticed the difference.'

'We believe,' said the General, 'that they have infiltrated into the TV commercial market. And their primary aim is to get the public disorientated and distressed before taking over.'

I laughed all the way home. And then I started to watch a lot of TV commercials and I thought I dunno – they could be right. Talk about confusion: There's one that comes on regularly showing a feller arguing with a ref, another feller miscuing a billiard ball, a dog lying down, a girl fetching her boyfriend a whack around the gizzard, and the message comes up 'Drink Coke!' Can you make that out?

Commercials are definitely taking a *peculiar* turn. And how is it that washing powders are getting more and more powerful, almost by the hour, and our kids have never looked scruffier?

Are there insidious alien minds at work implanting the idea that we humans are inferior? Take that paragon of common sense, the average housewife. According to the message purveyed in TV commercials, she can't do a damn thing right.

No matter what she buys, whether it's toothpaste, coffee, soap powder, or washing-up liquid, a nosey old goat rushes in from next door, sneers all over her shopping bag, and tells her she's been using the wrong brand for years! The poor housewife can't escape from her. She pops up in cafés, hairdressers, and from behind stacking counters in supermarkets. The poor creature is turning neurotic, hiding things inside her shopping bag and glancing over her shoulder, expecting the KGB neighbour to leap out with a 'Haha! Caught you! Buying that shitty coffee!'

And in the long run that kind of harassment must start to affect her love life. How can she concentrate in bed if she's half expecting this harpy to leap in and shout, 'Don't tell me you're still using that old Kevin? Why not switch to Henry here? Feel how much softer he is, how much fresher he smells!'

There's also a big debate going on about sponsorship on television. As you know, athletes are powerless today unless they have sponsors. Take all the

brand names off a tennis player's shirt, shorts, and racket, and he plays stark naked.

Lack-lustre football teams have been known to leap to the top of the league as soon as they don strips with 'Toshiba' all over them.

Sport doesn't belong to us any more. It belongs to a group of people who flog booze, cars, and radios. It won't be too long before the next Coronation; when units of the Thorn EMI army lead the Whitbread's Coronation coach down to the Benson & Hedges Abbey for the monarch to be crowned by the Archbishop of Ariel Automatic.

But that is one good thing that will come out of television sponsorship. There will be no World War III because it will never find the sponsors. Nobody can afford a long war these days without sponsors. Look at the Israeli War: no sponsors and it was over in six days.

The Americans will find the sponsors, of course. They've got the lot. United Steel, Kraft cheese, Chevrolet cars, Kelloggs, the Chase Manhattan Bank . . . they're all dying to sponsor a war. 'This part of the battle was brought to you by Baked Wheatie Breakfast Foods. Stay tuned for the missile launch'.

But you can't fight a war on your own, and what have the Russians got? Bulgarian Zinc, Vladivostok Tractors, and Mongolian Manure. No TV station is going to buy those.

So we're pretty safe at the moment. Unless Pan Am decides to sponsor the Russians, and who believes that they wouldn't?

The BBC meanwhile stands aloof from all this. In theory they don't support sponsoring. In practice, they've got so many sponsors' names flashing on their sports' programmes, its getting pretty damn difficult to tell which side you're tuned into.

A friend of mine has run his car for thirty years without buying a tax disc. When the police are known to be active, he will compromise by sticking on a Guinness label. He's already some £4000 richer than I am, and if he remains undetected, he will die richer by twice that amount.

Another pal of mine has never bought a postage stamp; but his letters always get there. If he wants to send a letter to Allen Goodall, the Dorchester Hotel, he puts a fictional address on the front, and on the back writes 'If undelivered please return to Allen Goodall, the Dorchester Hotel'. The system hasn't failed yet. The British are a nation of Artful Dodgers. Pass a law and they'll find a dozen ways round it.

So that brings us to the TV licence dodgers, which in turn brings us to the Carrott Castbroading Company (Channel 5).

Successful negotiations have taken place to set up our own TV network as named above.

Our Demographic Team have been conducting an enquiry among 1000 viewers and the questionnaire elicited the following:

Question: WHAT DO YOU DISLIKE MOST ABOUT TELEVISION?
Answer: TELEVISION
Question: WHAT DO YOU *LIKE* MOST ABOUT TELEVISION?
Answer: THE TEST CARD.

In the end, we voted against showing the Test Card. It would inevitably incur the wrath of other channels showing their Test Cards, with accusations that we were deliberately starting a ratings war. Secondly, the Test Card would immediately attract a large fanmail, which we were not prepared to handle. We have therefore voted to show a blank screen for most castbroading hours, thus giving viewers exactly what they want.

This immediately altered our policy towards the TV licence dodgers. In fact reversed it. The majority of the public went on paying their licences and watching the programmes, even though they had registered their cynical view of it. They were traitors to their own cause.

The licence dodgers on the other hand, by not coughing up the necessary, were trying to bring television to a grinding halt, and putting their cheque books out on a limb in defence of their principles. We began to feel warm towards them. There they were, crouched in their homes, with detector vans circling them like Indians round covered waggons, stubbornly refusing to give in.

So our network has decided to castbroad a limited service to licence dodgers only, in token of their high moral aims. The first day's schedule works out as follows:

CCC Network Licence Dodger Service

8.00 a.m. Breakfast TV
Picture of a clock with a small inset of a presenter in the bottom left-hand corner. Plus a soundtrack from the speaking clock with sub-titles.

10.00 a.m. Watch With Childminder
A series of pictures featuring detector vans in all their different, cunning disguises (milk float, shopping trolleys, immense pigeons). When they're out playing, the kids can then recognize the danger and give prior warning.

1.00 p.m. Trouble at Pebble Mill
Featuring a man who collects shirt buttons with a maximum of two holes in them, an interesting recipe for toast and yet another visit to the Mill Garden to watch the grass grow.

3.00 p.m. Afternoon Fill-In
Gloria Hunniford interviews leading stars at Madame Tussauds. Sub-titles.

6.00 p.m. International News
Test Cards from Common Market countries and the Middle East.

9.00 p.m. Sportsnight
Highlights from the Amateur Chess semi-finals in Rotherham.

12.00 p.m. Close
A photograph of the dot that remains after you have turned the set off, with an accompanying high-pitched tone.

We also had to initiate a policy regarding the showing of 'repeats'.

As everybody knows, repeats are shown so that fans can see their favourite shows again. Also so viewers who missed a series' first airing have the opportunity of seeing it for the first time – a special concession to those who work unsociable hours. This is network-boss bullshit for 'We can't afford to do anything new, so we'll show something old again'.

The Carrott Castbroading Company will monitor the most popular blank hours shown and repeat them whenever possible.

CENSORED SCENES FROM MY AUTOBIOGRAPHY
DYLAN WAS MY ROADIE

The year was 1971. Edward Heath was in power. The Bay City Rollers were in the charts. There was a rumour going about that the sixties were over.

I was doing the folk clubs at the time. Nottingham, Birmingham, Skeggie. I had become well known for my soul-wrenching musical interpretations of life as a folkie doing the clubs in Nottingham, Birmingham and Skeggie. My finger-work was great, my lyrics unforgettable, and as for my Bob Dylan imitations . . .

It all started one fresh April evening. The phone rang. My wife answered it.

'Bob Dylan for you,' she said.

I picked up the receiver, my heart beating like the bass line in 'Leopard-skin Pillbox Hat'.

'Hey, Mr Jasper Carrott,' sang the familiar voice at the other end, 'Sing a song for me – '

'Hello, Bob,' I said uncertainly.

'I'm so weary and my feet are tired of wanderin' – '

He was some twenty minutes into 'Mr Tambourine Man' before I plucked up the courage to interrupt him.

'How can I help you, Bob?'

'Are you ready to go anywhere, are you ready for to fade – ?'

'Er – '

'Into my own parade?'

'We-ell – '

'Cast yer dancin' spell my way?'

'Of course, Bob but – '

'It's a deal, man,' he said, suddenly coming on like Mr Heavy Business-man. 'You're deppin' for me down Isle of Wight way, man. Get that old Bobby Dylan wig on, man, stuff some cotton wool up yer nose, untune that guitar 'cos you is top of the bill, man.'

As he launched into the chorus of 'With God On Our Side', several thoughts raced through my mind. They were:

1. This man is so far out to lunch that it's almost teatime.

2. I need the cash.

3. Surely even a brilliant impressionist like myself couldn't get away with impersonating Bob Dylan in front of thousands of fans.

4. Except they'll all be stoned out of their boxes anyway.

5. Dylan's voice sounds even worse over the phone than it does on his records.

6. I need the cash.

7. I wouldn't like to see his quarterly phone bill.

8. Maybe this could be my big break as a rock star – no more Nottingham, Birmingham, Skeggie.

9. I'll probably be sharing a dressing-room with Mick and Keith.

10. Do they have dressing-rooms at rock festivals?

11. Would it blow my cover if I asked for Mick and Keith's autographs?

12. Bloody hell, do I need the cash.

'I'll do it, Bob! I said . . .

It was the ultimate bummer, man. Heavy, like Cyril Smith. Freaky, like Yoko Ono. A bad trip, like a soccer special full of Millwall fans after a crushing away defeat.

When I arrived in my limo, the place looked like something between the Battle of the Somme and a mud-wrestling convention. Millions of very wet hippies were doing their best to partake in traditional hippy activities – getting stoned, taking their tops off, shaking their heads in time with the music, and generally kidding themselves they were having a good time.

There were queues everywhere. Some people had been queueing for so long that they'd forgotten whether they were queueing for the bog or the bad trips tent.

This made the bad trips tent a very unpleasant place indeed.

As I made my way through this nightmarish scene, escorted only by a dozen or so bodyguards, a sodden hippy emerged from his private, drug-befogged world long enough to recognize me.

'Hey man. Dylan man. Keep on truckin' man. Riiiiiiight on,' he said, before falling flat on his face in the mud.

This was going to be easy . . .

Those days, if you were anybody in the rock business, you didn't just appear on stage with your band. You had to have a few megastars jammin' in the background. Then you could say, 'Hey, Arlo, you wanna grab a little of this man?' and the place would erupt as some zonked-out half-forgotten hippy stumbled up to the microphone.

Trouble was, I was the only megastar around. And my only Dylan number was the first verse of 'The Times They Are A-Changin'.

In the end we told a couple of session musicians to act stoned as they played the guitar – they could be Keith and Eric – the drummer to put on a silly grin – he was Ringo – and gave the pianist a silly wig – he was Leon Russell. Finally we got hold of one of the technicians and with the help of a particularly violent exploding suppository, he did a very creditable impression of Mick Jagger.

We were a triumph . . .

According to leading Dylanologists, there have been five main phases to Bob Dylan's career:

1. His folk-singing phase.

2. His electrical rock phase.

3. His Eurovision Song Contest phase.

4. His Christian phase.

5. His return-to-my-roots phase.

Guess which phase my Isle of Wight gig launched?

Well, we had to play something and the band only knew 'Boom-Bang-a-Bang'. So I did a bit of Dylan rap about it being contemporary, subterranean, alternative comment on the Bomb and away we went – forty-five minutes of a headbangers' version of 'Boom-Bang-a-Bang'.

It was magic.

Years later, sharing a pipe with Bobby and his old lady in their six-storey mountain shack in Aspen, Colorado, Dylan told me that he now had to include 'Boom-Bang-a-Bang' in all his performances. These days he claims it's a contemporary, subterranean, alternative comment on Star Wars.

So we had a laugh, reached down for the guitars, and he tried to teach me the chords for 'Don't Think Twice' . . .

I suppose you want to hear about the famous Isle of Wight orgy there were all those rumours about.

The drinking race with Joe Cocker in a local swimming-pool filled with vodka.

Sonny and Cher's 'live show'.

The notorious nude mud-wrestling match between Joni Mitchell and Joan Baez.

Well, frankly, I have no time for that kind of filthy, public muck-raking. They may be showbiz megastars to you, but to me they're some of my closest personal friends.

My full and frank account of the steamy, no-holds-barred sex secrets of the stars – plus the candid, often shocking snaps I took at the time – will remain under lock and key until a responsible public newspaper makes me a *sensible* offer for serial rights.

Because all that's quite another story . . .

THE TEN MOST BORING LISTS

1. The ten most frequently ignored road signs.

2. The ten most desirable, conveniently situated, in need of slight modernization estate agents.

3. The ten least controversial telephone directories.

4. The ten most common uses for paper clips in an office environment.

5. The ten least endangered species in the world.

6. The ten most profound statements by pop stars on the fundamental meaning of existence.

7. The ten nicest fields in New Zealand.

8. The ten least instructive three-hour speeches delivered on May Day by a member of the Politbureau.

9. The ten most popular towns in Belgium.

10. The list of The Ten Most Boring Lists.

CARROTT CARDS

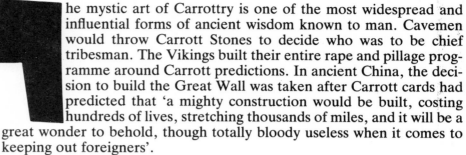

he mystic art of Carrottry is one of the most widespread and influential forms of ancient wisdom known to man. Cavemen would throw Carrott Stones to decide who was to be chief tribesman. The Vikings built their entire rape and pillage programme around Carrott predictions. In ancient China, the decision to build the Great Wall was taken after Carrott cards had predicted that 'a mighty construction would be built, costing hundreds of lives, stretching thousands of miles, and it will be a great wonder to behold, though totally bloody useless when it comes to keeping out foreigners'.

More recently, the use of Carrott cards have accurately predicted:

World War II ('Quite a big conflagration will descend upon the earth in the middleish part of the century, give or take a decade or two.')

The assassination of Kennedy ('The pearly-toothed swordsman shall have a bit of bad luck.')

The kidnapping of Shergar ('The swift-footed giraffe* shall stub his toe and fall.')

The marriage of Prince Andrew and Fergie ('The grinning birdman will leap the Canyon† to reach the other side.')

Today Carrott cards are used all over the world by leaders and persons of wealth and importance when they are faced with a tricky decision. They are to be found in the Oval Office at the White House and in the Vatican's revered Holy of Holies. In Britain, hardly a cabinet meeting goes by without the Prime Minister asking, 'Foreign Secretary, what say the Carrott Cards upon this issue?'

'They say that we should send the fleet, knock hell out of the Argies, and ride into the next election on a patriotic ticket, Prime Minister.'

'So be it. It shall be done.'

But Carrott Cards are not only for mighty affairs of state. They can help *you* plan *your* future, even if you are an insignificant little nobody. In fact, if you *are* an insignificant little nobody, then the Carrott Cards will be the first to tell you.

Here's how to use your customized, hand-tooled set of Carrott Cards:

Deface this book by cutting out the cards on this page.

Ask somebody you can trust, preferably a magistrate, vicar, or Commissioner for Oaths, to shuffle the pack and lay the cards face down on a table.

---

*Swahili for 'giraffe' is 'sige', which sounds quite like 'Shergar' when said very fast.
† 'Canyon' has been translated as 'hole' in some versions. This is believed to be a tangential reference to 'the mint with a hole', also known as 'Polo'. Fergie's father is, of course, a polo manager.

Select a card at random. Then ask the magistrate, vicar or Commissioner for Oaths to pick it up off the table *with the tip of his or her tongue.*

You should then endeavour to take the card from him or her using the tip of your tongue. If the card drops, repeat the procedure with another card of your choosing.

Once you have the Carrott Card on the tip of your tongue, blow hard through your mouth. If the card falls face down, the fates are at work once more and the entire procedure should start again.

Occasionally all five cards land face downwards. This means quite literally that you have such a dull life and future that it's a waste of anybody's time even discussing it. In this case, the Cards should never ever be used again except as bookmarks.

Here are your Cards, complete with the profound, mystical and utterly obscure character insights which have become legendary over the ages.

Remember – Carrott Cards never lie!

THE RUNNER

From the moment you arrived in this world, your life has been a race. You were a hyperactive child, much disliked by your parents, a swot, much disliked by your teachers, and, later in life, a breathless and overenthusiastic lover, much disliked by your other half. Sadly the 100-metre dash that is your life has got nowhere. While most people are more or less managing to get from A to B, you're trying – and failing – to get from A to 2. You'll never slow down now and, as you get older, your rushing about will become increasingly absurd and undignified. You'll finally get a break when you keel over mid-gasp and die of a coronary arrest. This will happen on 19 April 1989.

The Runner

The Rebel

THE REBEL

You are a monumental pain in the bum. In a restaurant you always want a table someone else has reserved. You always want plaice when they only have sole. You always quibble over the bill. Rooms empty when you walk in. If someone says 'Good morning', you'll find some reason to disagree with him. Deep down, you know you haven't got a worthwhile opinion in your head, so you try to make yourself interesting by whining, nagging and whingeing whenever you can. But divine justice awaits you. Next week, you'll go to the pub you've terrorized by your daily presence for the past three years and get into a fight with the barman, Del, an ex-police sergeant in the Special Patrol Group. After he's laid you out cold, you'll be revived by having Babycham squirted up your nose. That'll teach you.

THE CRAWLER

You surprised your parents by refusing to walk until the age of four and a half. Since then there's always been a stooped, apologetic look about you – you've long since forgotten how to start a sentence without first using the word 'sorry'. To be fair, you have got a lot to be sorry for. You don't look, for a start, and you've the sex appeal of a toad with a hump. You're going to be fired from your job soon (again!), and your spouse will leave you in disgust. You'll then move out to a dingy bedsit with tin ash-trays with 'Players No. 6' written on them, a black-and-white television and one gas ring. You'll probably live to a ripe (!) old age, but no one will notice.

The Crawler

The Prat

THE PRAT

You know how every pig litter has a runt? Well, you are one of life's runts. At school, you couldn't run, jump or skip to save your life. You were pathetic in class, and in the playground you were ignored except when they wanted a game of football. You were the ball. The question that used to be heard in those dim and distant days – 'Is there *anything* that prat can do?' – is rarely asked today. One glance at your ill-fitting clothes, shifty eyes and unfortunate, clammy skin says it all. Your future is a wasteland of social humiliation and sexual frustration. You might hang around for a few years, and then again you might not. It's not going to make much difference to the rest of us either way.

THE REAPER

Good Lord, are you still around? According to our records, you should have shuffled off this mortal whatsit ages ago. Still, look on the bright side – since you're living on borrowed time, you can afford to behave in a really wild, devil-may-care sort of way. Why not play dodgems on the motorway or juggle with a couple of chainsaws at full throttle? You'll be going soon so why the hell don't you go in style? As soon as you've finished reading this, the best thing you could do is draw up a will. You haven't got much to leave, but it shows that even a diehard like you occasionally thinks of others. Try not to break down when you read this. A lot of people believe in reincarnation and – who knows? – there might even be an afterlife. Mind how you go.

The Reaper

CARROTT'S BAD HOTEL GUIDE

ince I spend great chunks of my peripatetic existence in hotels, I'm always looking for the perfect hotel – great food and service, lavish surroundings, and exotic settings at about £10 per night. Needless to say, I have yet to come across it. The horrendous hotel depicted in 'Fawlty Towers' for all its exaggeration is the role model for many similar establishments spread round the country.

There are, however, other classifications of hotel that as yet have not been made into a TV series. So here for the would-be John Cleese/Connie Booth is a guide to other types of hostelry.

The Ultra Modern

This class of hotel is totally devoid of humanity and, where automation is not possible, it gets you to do the work.

On arrival you put your bags on a conveyor and park the car yourself. This is not easy because hotels of this nature are beloved by management executives, salesmen, etc., who can play all sorts of fiddles with their expenses because there's no one there to check. Two in a room – drinks made out to phone calls, etc. The car park is awash with Sierras, Cavaliers and Granada coupés with sun roofs.

Entering the foyer you find the reception is entirely automatic. Slip your credit card into a slot and the pre-arranged computer issues you with a metal-impregnated cardboard key with your room number on and wishes you a happy stay in a pre-recorded voice that sounds like a Dalek with a harelip.

As you punch your room number into the conveyor-belt computer, your baggage is whisked away to your room. You walk to the lift and *you* are whisked away to meet your baggage.

Entering your room you are met by twelve sales reps who have also been given the same room as yourself. Their luggage too has been deposited in the same room – along with everyone else's who's checked in the same day.

Several of the reps are trying to stay alive by attempting to activate the automatic food and beverage dispenser. The oxtail soup, meat pie and Black Forest gâteau have arrived with a distinct lack of food content, but at least there's plenty of hot water.

By bedtime the numbers of guests in the room have swelled to well beyond thirty, grateful for the fact that there are plenty of suitcases to sit on. The luggage keeps on arriving, but by turning the wardrobe on its side and jamming it up against the conveyor door you get a temporary respite. The cool air conditioning is very useful at this stage as it keeps suffocation to a minimum, but there are one or two victims of frostbite whose cries of acute pain would be very distressful except that they're drowned out by the noise of the air conditioner.

At 6 a.m. the next morning the only human employee allowed on the premises, the cleaner, turfs us all out because she wants to make the bed.

Hotels like this are usually called 'The Sleek Accountant' or 'Ye Olde Sales Report'.

The Faded Glory in the Middle of a City Slum

This sort of hotel was built when Cromwell was just learning to eat Farley's Rusks. As the years went past, the landed gentry and ludicrously rich patrons moved out of the cities and into the country. Terraced houses, known as derelict hovels in the centre and bijou residences in the villages, now surround the once proud turrets and buttresses of the hotel entrance.

With all these sort of hotels no one will actually ever admit that times have changed and the routines and ways of old are still adhered to.

When you arrive at the Faded Glory, it costs you a small fortune before you even step over the threshold. The first people you meet are the local junior mafia (average age nine) who politely enquire whether they may guard your car in case anything untoward may happen to it. A refusal guarantees that something 'untoward' *will* happen and £5 will restrict the damage to a very low tow-away fee.

The doorman is quite frequently an outcast from professional wrestling for frightening the crowd. He has security identity all over him because it has been known while he's helping a guest unload his baggage someone dressed up as a porter steps into his place and walks off with the next punter's complete set of suitcases.

The hotel itself is a haven for a couple of dozen varieties of spider. Local schoolchildren are taken round on nature studies and collect different samples of web to take home and knit jumpers.

The staff consist of two sorts only; so old they helped to build the place or YTS youngsters straight from school. The youngsters are very inexperienced and are quite likely to serve the coffee in a bed warmer. What they are training for is debatable, and they probably sussed out long ago that as convenient labour fodder in six months' time they'll be back on the streets protecting cars.

At least there is a chance that when you order breakfast from one of these youngsters you will get it. Not so for the older staff. It's very difficult carrying a breakfast tray using a walking frame. More often than not halfway up the landing they forget which room they're going to, and return with the full tray to the kitchen thinking they've cleared up and collected it from the room.

It is impossible to order anything else for breakfast in these establishments except a Henry VIII banquet feast. They've never heard of a continental breakfast, in fact, they've probably never heard of the continent.

You use the restaurant at your peril, starvation being slightly more preferent than being talked to death by the head waiter reminiscing about the First World War.

There are useful things you don't get in normal hotels; toilet seats that stand up, baths you can actually sit in without getting cramp. There are places to tie your horses, wig racks and if you leave your shoes outside the door, well, you need your head looking at.

These hotels are usually called 'The Adelphi', 'The Connaught' or 'The Grand'.

The Rip-Off Joint

My experience of these establishments is very limited. Primarily, the understanding is you do everything yourself but tip generously anything that moves with epaulettes.

You pay for everything. Phone down to reception to enquire why the TV doesn't work and the call costs you the same amount as the man wants to repair it – £5. The hotel never charges anything less than £5. And if you go to the bar you have to think long and hard whether to buy a round or a villa in Marbella.

These hotels are frequented by the oldest profession. It's really an interior kerb crawl and, if you do make it to your room without being accosted, sleep is very difficult because in the room either side the night's work is in progress and you get coital stereo. Hotels like this trade under names such as 'The Winchester House', 'The American Plaza' or 'Glitz International'.

The Family-Run Establishment

These sort of hotels are easily recognizable because basically they scare the living daylights out of you. They are set in dark, forgotten corners of villages or towns and any one of them could have been the setting for *Psycho*. You're generally too petrified to take a shower.

The advertising blurb stresses that the hotel is completely family-run and that's precisely what they mean.

At the reception you are greeted by the three-year-old daughter who checks you in with her Cindy typewriter, and then your luggage is taken up to your room by the family German Shepherd. If your luck's in he won't have an aversion to leather, if it's out – I do believe you have a legal right to shoot him.

The bedroom is always extremely personal. It's quite obvious they've moved one of the family out of the room to accommodate you. There's photos of the family at Rhyl, every major pop star in the world is staring down at you from the walls, and a plaque on the outside of the door warns anyone of adult bearing that this room is Mandy's so why don't you push off?

A sure sign of one of these hotels is that they have a son who is a general dogsbody. And there's always the feeling that this son is a shade 'out to lunch'. The lights are on, the doors are open but he's just one can short of a six-pack.

Invariably he's the cook and cleaner. As you watch him scour the bathroom clean with gravy browning it does cross your mind what he makes the soup with. These sort of people also hover. It seems wherever you are in the hotel they are there, hovering. Disconcerting, I think, is the word. What do they want to see or do to you? Hovering in my opinion should be banned in hotels.

You might wonder when you stay in these places where the parents are. These people are rarely seen. The matriarch is always in the garden growing vegetables under cloches, while the old man is out trying to shoot ravens for dinner.

One doesn't stay too long in this sort of establishment – about one night is the average. As you dash away next morning, the whole family including the dog gather round to hover and see you off. Hotels like this are called 'Chez Hotel', 'Hotel de la Dun Romin' or 'Veracolin'.

ASTROLINES

CAPRICORN

A Capricorn's lot is a tough one
It's the sign of the goat you will find
They're stubborn and dim
With a compulsory whim
To butt people in their behind.

THE ADVENTURES OF BUZBY ON THE TELEPHONE

Book One. Buzby Gets Wired!

'Ho-hum,' said Buzby one day. 'Today's a special day. A *very* special day.'

'And why's today so special?' asked Loppity Rabbit, who happened to be hopping by at the time.

'Because,' said Buzby, 'tomorrow is Ting-a-Ling's birthday.'

'That means *tomorrow*'s a special day,' said Loppity. 'And today is the day before a special day.'

'Oh, you brainless bunny,' laughed Buzby. 'Today's so very, very, very special because I'm going to town to buy a telephone. Then I can ring Ting-a-Ling to tell her I'm coming to her special birthday party.'

'Dream on,' said Loppity, and hopped off.

Buzby put his fluffy little head to one side.

'I wonder what he could mean by that,' he said.

*   *   *

Telephone Tel was having a busy day in his shop. Some naughty person had mixed up all his telephones and now he was in the most terrible muddle.

'Ho-hum,' chuckled Buzby as he entered the shop. 'Today's a very special day.'

'Leave it out, mush,' said Telephone Tel. 'Someone's only gone and mated me Donald Duck mouthpieces with me Mickey Mouse receivers. So not so much of the special day, all right.'

'They look okay to me,' smiled Buzby. 'What exactly is wrong with them?'

Telephone Tel looked at Buzby for several moments in a thoroughly nasty way. He *was* a crosspatch today.

'Know someone who wants to buy a Mickey Duck phone, do you?' he sneered.

'As it happens I do,' chirped Buzby merrily. 'Me.'

Telephone Tel stared at him.

Then he stared at him some more. He stared and he

stared and he stared.

'Get away,' he said eventually. 'You want to buy a telephone?'

'Yes I do,' said Buzby, 'and one of your Mickey Ducks will suit me just fine.'

'I expect you want to use one of British Telecom's brand new facilities,' said Telephone Tel. 'Like Dial-a-Nursery Rhyme – '

'Nope.'

'Or Dial-a-very-old-Irish-joke?'

'Nope.'

'Then you must be interested in our new super hi-tech range. Questionphones that

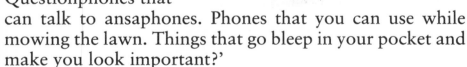

can talk to ansaphones. Phones that you can use while mowing the lawn. Things that go bleep in your pocket and make you look important?'

'Nope.'

'Then what do you want a telephone for?' asked Telephone Tel.

'I want to make a call to Ting-a-Ling.'

Telephone Tel's jaw dropped. Oh dear. Oh dear, oh dear, oh dear. What a prize chump he had here. What a silly old nincompoop. What a complete and utter divot.

'Ah yes, of course, sir,' he said. 'Make a call, sir. An excellent idea. And what a wise choice you've made with our new Mickey Duck model.'

*   *   *

'Sorry I couldn't make it before,' gasped Buzby as he arrived at Ting-a-Ling's cosy treetop home.

'What kept you?' squeaked Ting-a-Ling.

'I had to make a call,' said Buzby.

'A call?' said Ting-a-Ling. 'Who did you want to call?'

'You. I wanted to say I could come to your special birthday party.'

Ting-a-Ling scratched her cute little head.

'But my party was six months ago,' she said.

'It took me three months to be connected. Then my Mickey Duck's head fell off. Then I got nothing but wrong numbers, crossed lines and obscene calls. Then they cut me off for not paying my bill.'

'Oh deary me,' said Ting-a-Ling who really was the friendliest of creatures.

'And then I discovered you weren't even on the phone,' wailed Buzby.

'Why should I want to be on the phone?' asked Ting-a-Ling.

'Well,' chuckled Buzby. 'It makes life so much easier.'

The two pals laughed and laughed and laughed. . . .

THE END

OTHER CENSORED SCENES FROM MY AUTOBIOGRAPHY

TO BE RELEASED ONLY WHEN THE OFFICIAL SECRETS ACT ALLOWS

Above: 'I am the first person to get Hitler's autograph.'

Right: 'I am the mystery sub who really scored Geoff Hurst's goals in the World Cup final.'

Below: 'I make an honest woman of Jackie Aristotle Onassis/Kennedy after years of close friendship.'

Left: 'My early morning jogging pays off.'

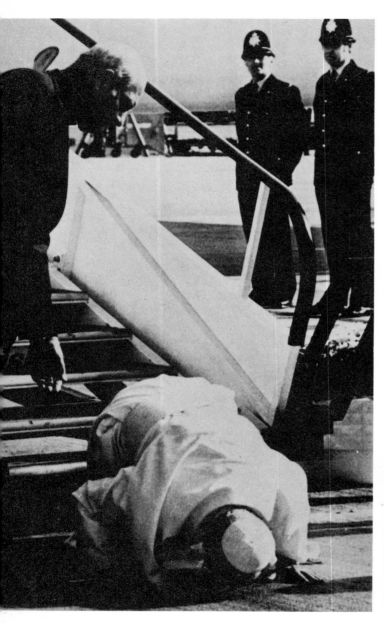

Right: 'I agree to join the Royal Family to help boost its popularity ratings.'

Above: 'My 1982 charity world tour on behalf of the Roman Catholic Church takes the Vatican to the top of the world religion charts for the first time since 1562.'

CALLING ALL FUDDY-DUDDIES!!!
ARE **You** between **38** and **50?**
Do YOU like to 'hit the sack' before 10.30 most weekdays?
Would YOU list 'DIY', 'watching television' and 'keeping regular bowel movements' among your interests?
Then pack up your bedroom slippers and come and join us.

Fuddies

Nice comfy beds with clean sheets, two pillows and a plastic mattress cover

Cocktail bars serving pina colada and scampi in-the-basket, while some divot croons Billy Joel's greatest hits on the piano

The holidays for the not-so-young at heart. Yes, **everyone's** talking about **FUDDIES** because we're the people who give the middle-aged the chance to do precisely what they want on holiday — vegetate in peace, just like they do at home. Because at **FUDDIES,** we believe in letting the prematurely old and boring 'do their own thing'. In other words, **FUDDIES** holidaymakers can do anything they jolly well like just so long as they don't interfere with the enjoyment of other **FUDDIES** — after all, we don't want to wake the geriatric old codgers as they take their afternoon zizz, do we? You could be interrupting someone as they are dying. How would *you* like it?
So this year, remember FUDDIES — holidays for the terminally insipid.

Mr Kipling's excellent tea-cakes

English-style flush toilets

Decent breakfasts with proper egg and bacon, toast soldiers and liver pills

Bowls tournaments (prizes for everyone!)

Twisting contests*
Lounge-suit dinners with lots of after-dinner speakers

*All FUDDIES holidays have on hand at all times a doctor specializing in heart and hernia conditions.

KILLING IN AMERICA

suppose America has a fascination for any artist and, particularly since some of my influences from the beginning were American comedians like Bill Cosby, Shelley Berman, Bob Newhart and George Karlin, it interested me to see how my material would work there. I've always known that my own style was American-influenced, but the content was based on my experience in this country.

British comedians in America, it has to be said, are regarded as the lowest form of life. With two notable exceptions, the awareness of British humour in the USA is zilch. The exceptions are, of course, Benny Hill and 'Monty Python'.

The success of 'Monty Python' is curious. The show went out on the American Public Broadcasting Service without, as far as I can ascertain, the patronizing cuts that would make it easier for the TV-insatiated audiences to understand. This meant that great slabs of 'Python' were being viewed by people with not the slightest knowledge of what was going on. Thereby lies its success. It became 'in' to like 'Python', to the point that today Americans who don't understand a single sketch play lip-service to its hilarity. Out of interest, I occasionally ask these devoted followers which one of the cast was Monty Python. Most of them plump for John Cleese.

Benny Hill is another matter. Everyone knows who he is, and everyone has a definite opinion as to his laughter-inducing capabilities. The problem starts when the Americans come to see Benny Hill as the beginning and end of British comedy and all that that entails.

I decided that 1984 was going to be the year I'd go to America – having moved away from the folk guitar image and done a couple of years of 'Carrott's Lib', I had a range of material that I could confidently take to the American market. My attitude was that, whatever happened, it would at least satisfy that desire to work in America and I could well be a better comedian for the experience. I also felt it would be a real test of my ability. Shorn of familiarity and up against intense competition, I was interested to see how I would fare.

My entry on to the American scene was helped by a six-foot-six country and western singer who ran a music club in San Francisco. I had met Fred Martin in Hong Kong in 1981 at a concert at which we both appeared. In one of those blasé statements that people make, he said that if I ever wanted help in America, I should give him a call. To his surprise, my manager turned up on his doorstep some three years later, asking him where all the clubs were.

I had decided to go to America as a total unknown and not to pull any strings through the BBC or other contacts in this country, so it was a question of Fred trundling around the club in the Bay area to get me some bookings. The reason I wanted to work from the ground floor upwards was

that I knew that you can't just appear on American television without having an idea of what you are letting yourself in for. There are enormous differences in the language, and subjects that you couldn't touch.

Much of my British act was going to be meaningless out there. They've never heard of Manchester United. They know who Margaret Thatcher is – she's second in line to the Queen, of course – but as for Geoffrey Howe or David Owen, they might as well be laundromat engineers.

Comedy clubs in America are really no more than bars that put on comedy because it's cheap and popular. You may think that this makes it easy to get work. Far from it. The competition is fierce, and it was no easy job for Fred to sell in an unknown limey comic even if he did have a pedigree of gold albums and his own TV series.

Eventually he found an agent ready to take a chance, but first I had to do some daunting appearances at what they call 'open mike nights'. These were nights at comedy clubs where they put on unknown, green-gilled comics or sometimes the professionals who came to work out new material.

My attempt to educate the 250 million Americans that there was an alternative to the Python/Hill humour began at a club called The Other Café in front of thirty-three people.

I had to get up and do ten minutes, and I don't remember ever being as scared as I was on that night. It was like my tongue was stuck to the roof of my mouth with Evo-stick.

I can't say that it was the best performance of my life but I did enough in those ten minutes to realize that, although it wasn't going to be easy working in America, there was every chance of making a mark. And having overcome that immense obstacle, the second night was fine and, after a couple of weeks, I had a nice, tidy thirty-minutes of material that became the basis of the act for the coming shows.

I started to make real progress when I went into the actual booked spots, where you are one of three acts billed to appear before a decent-sized audience, and there I found that I could get down to some real work, developing my material. It must have worked because, by the time I left, I was booked back to headline these clubs and others up and down the West Coast. I had proved, if nothing else, that I could earn a living as a comic in America.

I was surprised by the material that went down well in America – and by what was a total flop. For instance, we are used to the idea of Welsh or Scottish comedians extracting the Michael out of the English, so I thought an Englishman poking a bit of gentle fun at the Americans could work. How wrong can you be. I got out in front of one audience and said, 'Well, you always know where the next world trouble-spot's going to be – it's where Reagan's just sent a peace-keeping force.' Silence? You could have read a book.

The most difficult aspect for me about working over there was the stereotyped attitude of the audience towards me. I was an Englishman, no accent, no class distinction, an ethnic minority. They expected me to act how they imagined an Englishman would act – you know, with that dry, cool, laconic wit, and reserved, composed delivery. The first ten minutes could be quite awkward as they tried to figure out if I was an American comic doing a bad impression of an Englishman or the genuine article.

The introduction did not help either. I always used to ask the compere for a low-key introduction – something like, 'We have an English comedian for you now, he's over here to say "Hello", please welcome' and so on. Oh no! *No one* ever gets a low-key intro in America. Every act, whether he's Bob Hope or No Hope, gets announced as if he was the Second Coming.

'Ladies and gentlemen, we have for you tonight Britain's number one comedian. He's sold millions of records and books, toured the world. He walks on water and is fantastically funny. Welcome – JASPER CARROTT!!!'

The applause would be frugal and reasonably indifferent. They'd heard it all before, and anyway if he's Britain's number one comic, what's he doing in this poxy little club in San Jose?

The Americans listen to comedy like they watch TV. If it doesn't grab them immediately, they tune out. As a result, American comedians are petrified of silence. That's why their delivery is garbled out at 100 m.p.h.,

---

There are so many things that are confusing in America; signs are one of them. I had a Corvette Stingray car and on the bumper there was a sticker 'Honk for Jesus'. Now 'honk' in England means to throw up. There are stickers here that say 'Honk if you're horny'. No way am I going to do that! People say, 'Oh, come round and pick us up. When you get outside don't ring the bell – just honk.' I mean, by the time you've picked up about four people you don't want to go out, do you?

Another thing too, erasers. In England we call them *rubbers*. I didn't know at the time that rubbers is a euphemism for prophylactic. So, totally innocently, I walked into an office supplies store in San Francisco and said, 'Good morning, can I have a rubber, please?'

'Are you one of those dickheads?' I'm asked.

'No, I just want a rubber.'

'Then why don't you try the drugstore?'

So I went to the drugstore and there's a woman behind the counter, but then there always is in that sort of situation, isn't there? 'Good morning,' I say. 'Can I have a rubber, please?'

'You just want *one*?'

'Yes, I don't make *that* many mistakes! Have you got one with a Mickey Mouse on the end that I can chew?'

It was then that she called the police.

and at times the subject matters skit about alarmingly trying to find a vein of humour the audience can relate to.

You'll be pleased to know that I didn't pander to that style of attention grabbing. I found that courage brought its own reward. Not only did I take my time and develop themes as I normally do but, for the sheer hell of it, I would leave great gaps in my set by going to the 'john' halfway through the act or walking to the bar and ordering a drink.

I found that, by the end of my stay, my own delivery was quite a lot sharper. I didn't attempt the American hard rap, but merely tightened up my own basic style to fit in with the audiences' concentration levels.

Of course, you have to be very careful to remember the differences in language – in comedy, the wrong word in the wrong context can throw everybody. So if you say, 'Someone's nicked my rubber' to an American, he'd think some joker had been scoring your contraceptive sheath with a knife.

There's a tremendous range of comics from all sorts of ethnic minorities. I knew a Chinese comic who used to say it was difficult doing his type of material because twenty minutes after an audience had heard it, they wanted to hear it again.

Many of the local performers were interested in what I was doing and, by the end of my six-week stay, a lot of the established comics in the Bay area came over specifically to see me work. This gave me the opportunity to meet them and discuss comedy on both sides of the pond. I have to say

they were most helpful and encouraging, as well as being a great monitor for what was funny and what wasn't in my British material.

Yet, while there's a great camaraderie, once you get on stage it's 'dog eat dog'. There are no holds barred. Everybody goes all out to upstage the next person. In America, you have to pull out all the stops to raise the audience to fever pitch – to 'kill' as they say. If you don't 'kill', you can go down a couple of notches in the league. Not that it's always easy. The first time that I played the Improv Club in Los Angeles, there were about twenty-three people there, seventeen of whom were Japanese. But like a true professional, I had some material for the occasion and I told them about the problems of being a kamikaze pilot. You know, just as you're about to hit the ship, the bandana slips over your eyes and you miss it. So

I was walking through Central Park one Sunday morning last summer. It seems every 'crazy' in the world goes to Central Park on a Sunday morning. Well, to cut a long story short, when I was there, I didn't know what 'snow' was. I know what it is *now* but, of course, I didn't know *then*. There I was walking through Central Park, minding my own business, and there's a guy standing by a park bench and he said, 'Hey, Honkey!' I looked around for somebody throwing up. 'Yeah, you, come here, come here. Do you wanna buy some snow, man?'

Buy some snowman? I wondered where he'd been educated. Really, I was very intrigued. I said, 'How much?' 'Two thousand dollars an ounce!' Well, it was *August*, he'd probably been keeping it in his fridge or something. But I mean, two thousand dollars an ounce!

'But I can't afford that, I haven't any money,' I said, 'Look, you come over to England in January and we can really clean up. It just falls from the skies.' He called me a 'mother'. I've heard John McEnroe say that so I thought it must be a good word that.

He's good at expletives, John McEnroe, he's great. We learn at least six new words every time he comes to Wimbledon – particularly the umpires . . .

you have to return to base and go home to your ma and, when you knock on the door, she's really distressed. 'What on earth are you doing back alive?' she says, 'You just wait till your father gets home.' So you decide to do the honourable thing and commit hara-kiri, but even that's difficult because just as you've plunged the knife into your solar plexus, doesn't the phone always ring?

Possibly my most disastrous show occurred when Caesar's Comedy Store in Lake Tahoe decided that, after I had headlined successfully for five nights, they would put on a late extra show on Sunday night. It wasn't advertised very well, the two acts before me died the death and, by the time I got on at 1.30 in the morning there were precisely eight people out there. I was booked to do an hour, but ended up doing twenty minutes. Nobody cared much except me – in fact, most of the punters thought it was British humour and went back to the gambling machines.

Ten days later the same sort of thing happened in Portland, Ohio. Only this time I had worked out what I was going to do when confronted with this kind of situation. I got on at 1.45 and there were seventeen people there, extremely bored because the previous two acts had certainly failed to 'kill'.

However, even the prospect of a puerile British comic droning on for forty minutes can be something to look forward to in Portland. Having thought long and hard as to how I would approach the Lake Tahoe gig if it happened again, I was well prepared for this one. I ended up performing for well over forty minutes – an hour and a quarter, in fact – with an encore!

I was very proud of that performance, and any comic reading this will know exactly what I mean. 'Dying the death' is always a helpful experience – without going through that, you never really learn anything. Appearing before seventeen people in the small hours of the morning in Portland,

I was driving down 101 South in the Corvette and doing about 120 m.p.h. for the last ten minutes and the police in America, they don't mess about. Talk about quick. They were there in no time at all. Well, I braked like mad and got down to about 54 m.p.h., just poodling along, and they drove up alongside me.

Now I'm used to the *English* police, a totally different breed of men altogether. For example, if you go to England and see a policeman with three stripes on his arm it means he can read and write. If he's got two stripes it means he can *either* read or write, and if he's got one stripe it means he *knows* someone who can read or write.

When the police stop you in England, it's all so different; they're so polite and formal – though they can be very sarcastic in their own way. They'll pull up in front of you, get out and they'll put their hat on, walk up to your car and say, 'Good afternoon, sir' and 'Who's been a naughty boy then?' You've got to go along with it. 'Me, officer?'

'How naughty have you been?'

'Ever so naughty?'

Not here in America though – oh no. When the police get you on the hook, don't they play around with you, eh? They drove by the side of me for maybe two or three miles. There were two cops in the car, one of them arm on the sill, just staring at me. Suddenly he shouts, 'Hey, Knight Rider, pull over, pull over. Keep your hands where we can see them.' My hands were on the steering wheel anyway, they weren't going anywhere.

So I pulled over on to that hard shoulder that they have there with all the pot-holes and the dead cats, etc. The thing is, in England the police always pull up in front of you; well, in this country they always pull up behind. So I was just driving along waiting for them to overtake me, and they were driving behind waiting for me to stop. So for about ten miles we were just driving up and down.

Eventually, they got fed up and drove up alongside me.

'What the hell are you doing? Pull over, you dickhead!'

So I pulled over, wound the cellophane down and the next thing I know is I've got a six-gun in my ear.

'Right, okay Buddy, get out.'

Now, I've never had a six-gun in my ear before, I've had a few other things but never a six-gun. Please don't pull the trigger, I'm think, I've just had my hair cut.

'Get out.'

'Okay, okay, okay, okay.'

So I lifted the door off.

'What the hell do you think you're doing?'

So I thought I'd better say the right thing, 'About 120 miles an hour.'

'Ah, a comedian eh?'

'*Yes*, how did you know?' . . .

Ohio may seem a touch masochistic but it's all part of the learning process.

Valuable as the American experience was, the most important gain was to have done it. Having been through that, I now realize several important factors which have tempered my ambitions in America.

Going back to square one and starting all that touring, working the clubs, TV chat-show spots and spending inordinate amounts of time away from home frankly does not appeal. The comedy club grassroots system has its drawbacks. It is becoming so commercialized and competitive that the comics are afraid to take chances and creativity is being stifled.

I have to say that, even if success came in a big way, the best I could do in America would be to work on three cylinders. Because of the language difficulty, I could never be totally confident on stage – the ability to ad-lib is curtailed and for me that is where much of my new material comes from.

One of the first things I did when I got to San Francisco was to rent a car, which is pretty pointless really because though you can drive anywhere you want to there you can't park the bloody thing. You just drive round looking for car-parking spaces. The only place you can stop is at gas stations – to get more gas to go round looking for parking spaces. Everywhere you go to, every road sign points to Oakland. I ended up there too with another 30,000 cars all wandering round saying, 'Where the bloody hell are we?' There are cars in Oakland with skeletons in, and people wailing 'Get me outta here' and screaming hysterically 'I want to go back to San Francisco.'

I used the car-rental company called 'Rent-a-Wreck'. They should warn tourists about this. I thought 'Rent-a-Wreck' – that's a nice, trendy title, I'll use that, not realizing that is exactly what they *rent*. I rented a Corvette Stingray. It was a three-wheeler, cellophane in the windows, etc. They tried to get me to rent a Pinto at seven dollars a week, and when I asked what the catch was they told me that the fire-proof suit is 400 dollars a week extra.

In England a Corvette Stingray would be a dream car. You don't get your hands on one of those so easily, and I couldn't wait to try it out. Those cars really want to go, vroom, vroom, vroom, and I hadn't even turned it on.

I'd rented a small apartment in Greenwich Street and I'd parked the car overnight outside the apartment. Me, I know nothing. I'd parked it facing the wrong way for a start. Straight wheels too, on a street-cleaning day opposite a fire hydrant. I woke up the next morning and there's the car surrounded by cops who were just slapping tickets on it right, left and centre.

Anyway, I thought, today's the day I'm going to try it out, so I took the Stingray out on to 101 South. Well, Union Square was a bit busy. The trouble is in America you have this blanket 55 m.p.h. speed limit. There's me with a Corvette Stingray – you can't get it out of first gear at 55 m.p.h.! So I thought, what shall I do? Oh, what the hell, I'm only here for a couple of days, if I get stopped by the police I won't pay the ticket, sod them.

Off I went then, tearing along like mad, and I suddenly thought, what the hell's going on? I've got a four to five G force on my face, cellophane flapping in the wind, I'm dodging in and out of the traffic – of course, I'm driving the wrong bloody way, aren't I? In and out I'm going, cars honking and hooting at me, people shouting, 'What the hell are you doing?' and I'm saying, 'I'm English, pal, English.' What else *can* you do?

I'd been to Caesar's in Lake Tahoe, which is a big gambling area in case you didn't know. It was – as we say in England – 'gob-smacking'. We have nothing like it over there. Well, we *do* have gambling – it's called eating in restaurants. I mean, you can order a rare steak and what you actually get is a charcoal brickette. In fact, people order a steak and then they have to send it back because there's still some flavour left in it!

A couple of observations here about Caesar's though. That gambling, it really gets to you. You could be a Mormon, but within two days you'd be sticking money in those machines.

And it's wonderful to see the English there, especially those demure English ladies. You can hear them say, 'Oh hello,' and 'Oh, I'm not going to gamble, oh *no*, not me.' You can always tell they're English because their husbands are with them, and he's the chap who looks as though he's trying to grow a chin. You have to watch them because it really is funny. She'll say things like, 'Well, I'll just try *one little quarter*, tee hee hee' and 'Isn't this spiffing fun?'

Then you go back to her three hours later and there she is with about four cigarettes on the go shrieking, 'Does this shit machine ever pay out . . .'

MALE WATCHING

A Species by Species Guide

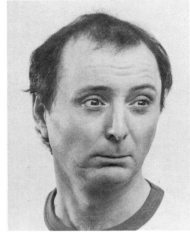

The Pinheaded Hulk

Species: Bird of prey
Habitat: Anywhere with flashing lights, coloured mirrors, Shalamar records and pina colada on tap
Plumage: Fancy jewellery and a chest toupee (optional)
Mating call: 'Hey, little doll, wanna do your body a favour and give my water bed a trial run?'
Migratory pattern: Summer migration to holiday resorts that were in fashion two years ago
Degree of rarity: Once common, but now threatened by universal ridicule

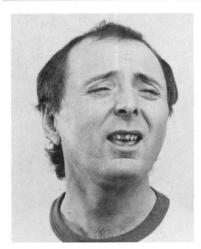

The Greater Honking Hooray

Species: Warbler
Habitat: London and the Home Counties
Plumage: Twenty or so handmade suits put together by a little man round the back of Harrods
Mating call: 'I say, Sarah, you don't fancy tooling on back to my pad for a spot of horizontal jogging, do you?'
Migratory pattern: Winters in St Moritz. Summers in St Tropez
Degree of rarity: Once scarce. Now growing in numbers

The Gawping Boggler

Species: Gannet
Habitat: Universal
Plumage: Torn tee-shirt and jeans at half-mast
Mating call: 'Goooooooooooooooo-eeeeeeeerrrr'
Migratory pattern: To its nearest watering hole at seven. Returns by indirect route later that night
Degree of rarity: Common

The Lesser Spotted Nerd

Species: Tit
Habitat: Milton Keynes and other new towns
Plumage: Grey, baggy and heavily stained
Mating call: Is not thought to mate
Migratory pattern: One outing weekly to the nearest Little Chef
Degree of rarity: Reasonably common, but rarely found in company

The Bureaucrat Bird

Species: Cage bird
Habitat: Happy anywhere there's a desk, a phone and other birds to boss around
Plumage: Head to toe Burtons the Tailors
Mating call: 'Please will you marry me?'
Migratory pattern: On the 8.21 in the morning, the 5.37 in the evening
Degree of rarity: Now to be found virtually everywhere

AQUARIUS

*Of hippies, bizarre and
    various
I've had more than I can take
So to call this the Age of
    Aquarius
Must be some kind of mistake.*

LEO

*Leos are hard-bitten people
They keep messing with lions,
    I'm afraid.
They're found in the main
To enjoy all the pain
And books by the Marquis de
    Sade.*

17 South Fork Mansions

Rylett Avenue

Solihull

Michael Grade

Chief Honcho

The BBC

London

Dear Gradey

<u>Ref: TRAVESTY - the ultimate British soap</u>

I've now finished work on the series that's going to put your
Consortium right back in the ratings where it belongs.

It's called <u>Travesty</u>, and it will include the best of
American soaps with some great British home-grown talent.

I hope you agree this is a winner.

I'm the star by the way

Yours

Jasper Carroll

Jasper (JC)

CAST LIST

JC - a cruel, manipulating, randy millionaire who oozes power, sex appeal and comic genius.

SAMANTHA FOX - his secretary and occasional bed partner.

DEX - a handsome, square-jawed son-of-a-bitch who's insanely jealous of JC's incredible sex appeal and success with women.

SUE ELLEN - a drunken beauty. Occasional bed partner of JC.

ANDREW RIDGELEY - toy boy to Sue Ellen.

ALEXIS - a cruel, cunning, overpaid bitch who uses her raw sensuality to get more reaction shots than she deserves. Occasional bed partner of JC.

STEPHEN - a nice boy, deeply confused about his sexuality.

HARROD SAYLE - Alexis' bitter and twisted twin brother, an angry bullet-headed taxi-driver who talks big and swears a lot.

ANNA RAEBURN - a ruthless and ambitious cousin of Dex, who's secretly jealous of the airtime and REVEILLE exclusives that Alexis is getting. Occasional bed partner of JC.

THE KING OF MOGADONIA - a handsome zombie, played by Michael Praed in a deep trance.

THE SPITTING IMAGE RONALD REAGAN - not nearly as funny as the real thing.

THE DUCHESS OF ARGYLL - Not an occasional bed partner of JC.

EXTRAS

All those girls who run about giggling in their undies on the 'Benny Hill Show'. Frequent bed partners of JC.

EPISODE 1

1. EXT. DISTANT SHOT OF SOLIHULL'S HIGHEST BUILDING.

RAPID ZOOM INTO A TOP WINDOW IN THE SKYSCRAPER ON THE THIRD FLOOR TO -

2. INT. JC'S ENORMOUS OFFICE OVERLOOKING SOLIHULL.

JC IS AT HIS ENORMOUS DESK WITH HIS FEET UP. HE IS ON THE PHONE.

JC:

25...105...72

(HE CONSULTS HIS CALCULATOR.)

...no - make that 73...no - not in ten minutes, now y'hear!

(SLAMS DOWN THE PHONE.)

One day I'm gonna buy that takeaway!

SAMANTHA FOX:

Oooer, lor loveaduck, JC, you are a one -

JC:

Shut up and get me Sue Ellen -

3. INT. SUE ELLEN'S BEDROOM.

SUE ELLEN IS IN BED WITH DEX, HARROD SAYLE, ABOUT A HUNDRED

BOTTLES OF BEER, HER POODLE MEX.   HER HAIR AND MAKE-UP ARE

PERFECT.   THE ONLY WAY WE CAN TELL SHE'S AS A NEWT IS THAT HER

GORGEOUS LIPS APPEAR TO BE TOTALLY OUT OF SYNC WITH THE SOUNDS

COMING OUT OF THEM.   THE PHONE RINGS.

SUE ELLEN:
Wayell, if it ain't Mr Big Shot himself.   Am ah to assoom that

this is wan of yawer random chayecks on may, JC? Well let me

tayell you exayactly what ah'm a-doin -

4. INT.A ROOM IN SOUTH FORK MAISONETTE.

ANDREW RIDGELEY, LOOKING AT A PICTURE OF JC, SLOWLY OPENS A

DRAWER FROM WHICH HE TAKES A REVOLVER.   HE PUTS IT IN AN INSIDE

POCKET AND WALKS OUT OF THE ROOM, SMILING PRETTILY.

5. EXT. IN FRONT OF SOUTH FORK MAISONETTE.

ANDREW RIDGELEY GETS INTO HIS CAR AND DRIVES OFF AT TOP SPEED.

HE CRASHES INTO THE GATE POST AT THE END OF THE DRIVE.   POIGNANTLY,

WE HEAR THE SOUND OF THE CAR RADIO COMING FROM THE BURNING WRECK.

IT'S PLAYING 'WAKE ME UP BEFORE YOU GO-GO'.

6. INT. JC'S OFFICE.

JC:

(SLAMMING DOWN THE PHONE.)

She's in bed, drinking Becks, with Dex, Lex and Mex -

SAMANTHA FOX:

Having - ?

JC:

A nice conversation. She says -

SAMANTHA FOX:

What you gonna do now, JC?

JC:

Shut up. I ain't givin' away my storylines for not nobody nohow,
not even you, you purty little thang. Now how's about you and
me -

CUT TO:

7. INT. LOUNGE-DINER AT SOUTH FORK MAISONETTE.

IT'S BREAKFAST TIME. THE DUCHESS OF ARGYLL IS POURING TEA FOR
ALEXIS, STEPHEN, ANNA RAEBURN AND THE KING OF MOGADONIA.

STEPHEN:

Hot dog, grandma, this sure is scrummy, crispy home-made rye
bread. I guess you wouldn't have the recipe for me some place?

ALEXIS:

(MIXED EMOTIONS COURSING ACROSS HER FACE, PLAYING HAVOC WITH

HER MAKE-UP.)

And what exactly would a grown man be needing a recipe for, may

I ask?

STEPHEN:

Well, it'd be just dandy if I could, y'know, try it out one

morning on Johnny. He just <u>loves</u> me to bring him a really neat

hot tea with English muffins in the morning and the papers, and

then we can just <u>cosy</u> up together all morning like two cutesy

little peas in a pod, y'know.

(THEY ALL LOOK AT HIM IN AMAZEMENT.)

Oh sugar, guess I done it again, huh?

ANNA RAEBURN:

Listen, love - isn't it about time you began to come to terms

with your own basic, inner sexuality. Why not wake up tomorrow

morning, look in the mirror and say, 'Hi, me - I <u>like</u> you - even

if you are a screaming Democrat!'? Call us back and tell us

how you got on, okay?

THE DUCHESS OF ARGYLL:

Excuse me - do I say my line yet?

ENTER JC.

JC:

There's a minor pop star scattered all over the drive. Anybody mind?

ALEXIS:

(MIXED EMOTIONS COURSING ACROSS HER FACE. ONCE AGAIN COMPLETELY SCREWING UP HER MAKE-UP WHICH ONLY TOOK LIKE THREE HOURS TO DO THIS MORNING.)

Andrew!!!!

ANNA RAEBURN:

Listen love, that's entirely healthy to your own grief situation. Never be afraid of letting go -

ALEXIS:

Right, that's it. If this uppity bitch is gonna screw my big scene, you can whistle for Alexis when it comes to the next series -

ANNA RAEBURN:

(CHOKING.)

The coffee...who put...

(FALLS UNDER THE TABLE.)

EVERYBODY LOOKS AT JC.

JC:

Why is it that, whenever anything goes a little bit wrong, everybody looks at me? Don't give her mouth-to-mouth, by the way -

THE KING OF MOGADONIA:

Why? The poison?

JC:

No, no but just look at her -

THE KING OF MOGADONIA:

(WINCING.)

I guess you're right -

THE DUCHESS OF ARGYLL:

I think you've gone past the bit where I say my line -

CUT TO:

8. INT. CLOSE-UP OF THE SPITTING IMAGE RONALD REAGAN

THE SPITTING IMAGE RONALD REAGAN:

My fellow Americans, we have reached the stage of the programme

where, every week, we make the same joke about me being old and

stupid. Then, if that doesn't work, we open my head or pull off

my nose, just like...this!

(HE PULLS OFF HIS NOSE.)

Great satire, huh?

9. EXT. THE COMMUNAL GARDEN OF SOUTH FORK MAISONETTE. IN THE

BACKGROUND IS A SWIMMING POOL.

THE ENTIRE CAST, EXCLUDING JC BUT INCLUDING ALL THE BENNY HILL

GIRLS IN THEIR UNDIES, ARE MILLING ABOUT IN FRONT OF THE POOL
MURMURING, LAUGHING, CHINKING THEIR GLASSES AND GENERALLY
PRETENDING THAT THEY'RE AT A PARTY.

HARROD SAYLE:

(TO NO ONE IN PARTICULAR.)

So I said to the soddin' advertising accounts manager, 'All
right, you crawly little Hampstead snot-nose, I'll do yer effin'
beer commercial but, just 'cos I'm pocketin' soddin' eighty
grand, don't expect me to abandon me effin' revolutionary
principles, right?

SAMANTHA FOX:

Has anybody seen JC? We can't do a swimming-pool scene without JC -

THE DUCHESS OF ARGYLL:

Excuse me, I'm waiting for my line -

STEPHEN:

Aren't we all, Sweetie. What kind of party is this?

ENTER JC. EVERYBODY FALLS SILENT.

JC:

This, Stephen, is the kind of party that doubles the budget and
adds a bit of random violence, sex and glamour to the dying
moments of the episode - that's what it is -

ALEXIS:

(MIXED EMOTIONS ETC., CAUSING THE MAKE-UP LADY TO RESIGN.)
But, JC how...????

HARROD SAYLE:

Don't think you're getting away with this, JC, you cunning,

brilliant, bastard.   (TAKES A SWING AT JC BUT MISSES.   IN THE

ENSUING MÊLÉE, MOST OF THE CAST FALL INTO THE POOL, WATCHED

COOLLY BY JC.)

JC:

That's how.   Now all we need is (HE STEPS TOWARDS SAMANTHA FOX,

WHO FALLS BACK INTO THE POOL) a bit of gratuitous titillation.

(SAMANTHA FOX STRUGGLES OUT OF THE SWIMMING POOL IN A WET T-SHIRT.)

STEPHEN:

(DRIPPING.)

But JC, what about the plot hook for next week's episode?

THE DUCHESS OF ARGYLL:

(FROM THE MIDDLE OF THE POOL.)

I've got it!   I've remembered it!

JC:

(IGNORING HER.)

Thank you for reminding me, Stephen.   You're (CLOSE-UP OF JC'S

ABSURDLY HANDSOME FACE.)

...pregnant?

THE CAMERA FREEZES ON JC BEFORE CREDITS START TO ROLL.

THE DUCHESS OF ARGYLL:

Would anybody like a nice cup of tea?

                    END

Le Body Language Français

A lot of people these days are simply frightened by the idea of going on holiday in France. They think that, just because the French are richer, happier, sexier and generally more sophisticated than the rest of the world put together, the foreigner will feel out of place there.

Not only that but they believe that the average Frenchman regards any effort to make him understand a foreign language as disgusting and totally immoral as, say, an attempt on the honour of his favourite daughter.

Now, thanks to Carrott's patent method Le Body Language Français, you can make that attempt on the honour of his favourite daughter – without actually saying a word.

Use the following gestures and most normal, red-blooded Frenchwomen will know exactly what you mean.

'Excusez moi chérie, but I could not help noticing you in your oh-so-chic French policewoman's uniform . . .'

'And I thought – why not? After all, was not L'Amour invented in this wonderful country of yours?'

'Because you are all woman, I am all man – together we could make sweet musique, know what I mean?'

'Don't worry about precautions, by the way – I'll pop into a chemist's on our way back to the camp site!'

'Okay, so we don't speak the same language – but why not let our bodies do the talking, hein?'

'All right, officer, I'll come quietly – *very* French and romantic, I must say. . .!'

ASTROLINES

ARIES

I like the average Aries
They replace children's molars
* with money.*
They're hirsute, and some
* things*
Called gossamer wings
Are what make 'airy fairy
* Aries so funny.*

ASTROLINES

PISCES

Everybody loves a Pisces
They love him head to toe.
Pisces are twice as nicese
Well if anybody I should
* know!*

JASPER

END PIECE

o,' thought Benny Hill to himself, 'I'm Prime Minister at last.'

He entered Number 10 Downing Street to take his place as the first ever leader of the Scantily Clad Party. His beliefs had been vindicated. The reason why people bought the tabloids instead of the pavement press was down to a basic desire for sleaze. Tap that instinct, mobilize the forces of erotica and the country would be his.

The topless policewoman gave Benny's bare behind a little squeeze as he slid past. If she wobbled and pouted enough, she thought, maybe he would notice her and take her on one of his constituency walkabouts. Mind you, you had to be fit for those, walking about at three times the speed of sound while smacking every bald-headed old dodderer in sight on the top of the head with an umbrella. But the effort was worth it just for the humiliation.

The bare-breasted officers were out in force (get it?!) today trying to hold back the surging crowd of SC party supporters. They were cheering wildly as Benny turned at the door to give them his cheeky grin and wave. The majority of them were men dressed in spotty underwear or Gannex raincoats, carrying placards which read 'WE WANT OUR MEMBERS EVERY-WHERE (*snigger*)' and 'STICK UP FOR YOUR RIGHTS (*snigger*)'.

There was one man in the crowd who wasn't cheering. As he surveyed the assembled mass with a professional eye, he felt strangely uncomfortable in his plainclothes attire of suspender belt and Playtex girdle. How he longed for his SAS khakis and the familiar feel of his M111 rifle. But for now his duty lay in the protection of the PM from the terrorist organizations pledged to de-bag Benny.

Suddenly there was an expectant buzz which began to swell (*snigger*) into an almighty roar. The Queen of Sleaze was approaching in an open-topped (*snigger*) double-decker bus. With her G-stringed minions cavorting salaciously on the top deck, she threw the crowds tantalizing glimpses of her own top deck (*snigger*). Slowly, seductively, she made her way down the stairs, disappearing temporarily from view only to reappear seconds later dressed only in a dazzling red sapphire inset into her navel.

The crowd as one started to roar her name – the name that had appeared on every front page of every paper in the world. The name that had been a household word since the early eighties. The name that had been associated with every chat-show host, soap-opera hero and quizmaster of any renown. And the name was –

TO BE CONTINUED . . .

In my next book, find out what happens to Benny, who is the Queen of Sleaze, and whether Fiona Richmond will be appointed Commissioner of Police.

Also more large-print chapters that end at the top of the page, illustrations that appear twice the size that they should and any other rip-off fill-in ideas that I can think of in the meantime.

ACKNOWLEDGEMENTS

Editor: **Terence Blacker**
Designer: **Alex Evans**
Assistant: **Zoltan Marfy**
Photographer: **Mike Prior**
Make-up: **Janet Rivaera**
Photomontage: **Sands Graphics**
Illustration: **David Stoten, Tim Watts** of Spitting Image
Typesetting: **Rowland Phototypesetting, Span Graphics**
Additional Photography: **Mark Westwood** (Wine supplement), **Laurentz Beckstead/Starward Productions** (Killing in America)
Picture research: **Diane Rich**
Archive photographs: **Associated Press** (pages 13, 40, 77, 94, 98), **Rex Features** (page 17), **Syndication International** (pages 47, 95, 99), **Allsport** (page 96)